A Note From Rick Renner

I am on a personal quest to see a "revival of the Bible" so people can establish their lives on a firm foundation that will stand strong and endure the test as the end-time storm winds begin to intensify.

In order to experience a revival of the Bible in your personal life, it is important to take time each day to read, receive, and apply its truths to your life. James tells us that if we will continue in the perfect law of liberty — refusing to be forgetful hearers but determined to be doers — we will be blessed in our ways. As you watch or listen to the programs in this series and work through this corresponding study guide, I trust that you will search the Scriptures and allow the Holy Spirit to help you hear something new from God's Word that applies specifically to your life. I encourage you to be a doer of the Word that He reveals to you. Whatever the cost, I assure you — it will be worth it.

Thy words were found, and I did eat them;
and thy word was unto me the joy and rejoicing of mine heart:
for I am called by thy name, O Lord God of hosts.
—Jeremiah 15:16

Your brother and friend in Jesus Christ,

Rick Renner

Unless otherwise indicated, all scripture quotations are taken from the *King James Version* of the Bible.

Christ's Message to Ephesus

1814 W. Tacoma St.
Broken Arrow, OK 74012-1406

Published by Rick Renner Ministries
www.renner.org

ISBN 13: 978-1-68031-619-3

eBook ISBN 13: 978-1-68031-657-5

How To Use This Study Guide

This ten-lesson study guide corresponds to ***"Christ's Message to Ephesus" With Rick Renner*** **(RENNER TV)**. Each lesson in this study guide covers a topic that is addressed during the program series, with questions and references supplied to draw you deeper into your own private study of the Scriptures on this subject.

To derive the most benefit from this study guide, consider the following:

First, watch or listen to the program prior to working through the corresponding lesson in this guide. (Programs can also be viewed at **renner.org** by clicking on the Media/Archives links or on our Renner Ministries YouTube channel.)

Second, take the time to look up the scriptures included in each lesson. Prayerfully consider their application to your own life.

Third, use a journal or notebook to make note of your answers to each lesson's Study Questions and Practical Application challenges.

Fourth, invest specific time in prayer and in the Word of God to consult with the Holy Spirit. Write down the scriptures or insights He reveals to you.

Finally, take action! Whatever the Lord tells you to do according to His Word, do it.

For added insights on this subject, it is recommended that you obtain Rick Renner's ten-part teaching series ***Christ's Message to Ephesus*** and his book ***A Light in Darkness: Seven Messages to the Seven Churches***. You may also select from Rick's other available resources by placing your order at **renner.org** or by calling 1-800-742-5593.

TOPIC

John's Divine Visitation

SCRIPTURES

1. **John 1:5** — And the light shineth in darkness; and the darkness comprehended it not.
2. **Revelation 1:1** — The Revelation of Jesus Christ, which God gave unto him, to shew unto his servants things which must shortly come to pass; and he sent and signified it by his angel unto his servant John.
3. **Revelation 1:4** — John to the seven churches which are in Asia: Grace be unto you, and peace, from him which is, and which was, and which is to come; and from the seven Spirits which are before his throne.
4. **Revelation 1:9-11** — I John, who also am your brother, and companion in tribulation, and in the kingdom and patience of Jesus Christ, was in the isle that is called Patmos, for the word of God, and for the testimony of Jesus Christ. I was in the Spirit on the Lord's day, and heard behind me a great voice, as of a trumpet, saying, I am Alpha and Omega, the first and the last: and, What thou seest, write in a book, and send it unto the seven churches which are in Asia; unto Ephesus, and unto Smyrna, and unto Pergamos, and unto Thyatira, and unto Sardis, and unto Philadelphia, and unto Laodicea.

GREEK WORDS

1. "companion" — (*sugkoinonos*): a companion; a joint-partner; two or more who mutually share the same place, principles, problems, tasks, or circumstances
2. "tribulation" — (*thlipsis*): affliction; trouble; great, crushing, suffocating pressure; a horribly tight, life-threatening squeeze
3. "patience" — ϖ μ (*hupomone*): to stay or abide; to remain in one's spot; to keep a position; to resolve to maintain territory gained; to defiantly stick it out regardless of pressures mounted against it; in a

military sense, it pictures soldiers ordered to maintain their positions even in the face of fierce opposition; staying power; "hang-in-there" power; the attitude that holds out, holds on, outlasts, perseveres, and hangs in there, never giving up, refusing to surrender to obstacles, and turning down every opportunity to quit; pictures one under a heavy load, but who refuses to bend, break, or surrender because he is convinced that the territory, promise, or principle under assault rightfully belongs to him; stamina; durability

4. "kingdom"— (*basileia*): a kingdom; a sphere of influence; ideology; even a political realm
5. "was"— μ (*ginomai*): to transition from one realm to another; indicates a sudden or surprising change — something unexpected that takes one off guard
6. "in the Spirit"— ϖ μ , , (*pneuma*): in spirit
7. "Lord's day"— (*kuriakos*): by the end of the First Century, it typically denoted the imperial day of the emperor; a day to worship the emperor; a significant function in the imperial cult of the emperor

SYNOPSIS

The ten lessons in this study on ***Christ's Message to Ephesus*** will focus on the following topics:

- John's Divine Visitation
- What Is the Church?
- Why Stars in Christ's Right Hand?
- Why Candlesticks?
- Doctrinal Integrity
- A Hard-Working Church
- How Does Anyone Leave a First Love?
- Remember
- What Is True Repentance?
- Who Were the Nicolaitans?

The emphasis of this lesson:

The apostle John was a living testimony of one who *started* and *finished* his God-given assignment. His life confirmed the ageless truth that "greater is He that is in you than he that is in the world" (*see* 1 John 4:4).

Although John experienced great tribulation and found himself in unexpected, undesirable situations, God never left him. And in what was perhaps this apostle's greatest moment of desolation, Christ brought revelation! The Holy Spirit empowered John to faithfully finish what God had told him to do. That is what God wants *you* to do. By His grace, you can finish your race, completing *your* God-given assignment on earth.

Just outside the city of Ephesus is the Basilica of St. John. The apostle John had moved to this location with Mary, the mother of Jesus, and lived there for several decades. After the apostle Paul was beheaded in 67 AD, John stepped into the primary leadership role of overseeing the churches in Asia. As he gave guidance to the churches, he also wrote the gospel of John along with the epistles of First, Second, and Third John.

At some point while living in Ephesus, John was arrested by Domitian and eventually banished to the isle of Patmos. It was there, amidst extreme, harsh conditions, that he found a cave in which to live. It was in this same cave that Jesus appeared to John, and it's where John wrote the book of Revelation.

After 18 months of John's exile, Emperor Domitian died. John, who was then in his 90s, returned to the city of Ephesus and lived out the rest of his life. The site of the Basilica of St. John was the original site of John's place of burial. Early in the Fourth Century, a massive cathedral was erected in John's honor at that very location. Although that cathedral now stands in ruins, that ancient site still marks the location of John's residence and original place of burial.

Writing about Jesus, John said, "The light shineth in darkness; and the darkness comprehended it not" (John 1:5). John had a revelation that darkness did not have the power to snuff out the light. The darkness did not and does not have the power to subdue, conquer, or take dominion over the light of Jesus!

The Revelation of Jesus Christ

The actual name of the final book of the Bible is "The Revelation of Jesus Christ." Notice what Revelation 1:1 says: "*The Revelation of Jesus Christ*, which God gave unto him, to shew unto his servants things which must shortly come to pass; and he sent and signified it by his angel unto his servant John."

The word "revelation" is the Greek word *apokalupis*, and it describes *something veiled or hidden that is now clearly seen*; it means *to remove the veil so that you can see what is there.* The revelation that John received was an unveiling of who Jesus is now — the risen King of Glory. What previously had obstructed John's understanding and perception of Jesus had been removed, and the true picture of Christ came into clear view for this devoted disciple.

Remember, John had walked and talked with Jesus for years. He carried many memories in his heart and mind of doing life with the Master. But in that Cave of the Revelation, as it is called today, John saw Jesus like he had never seen Him before. Jesus' human image was superseded by His glorified, kingly image. Through a supernatural move of the Holy Spirit, John suddenly received the revelation of Jesus as the exalted Christ, and he recorded it for all who would believe.

The Name 'John'

In Revelation 1, it is specifically noted in three verses that John was the one who was communicating this revelation of the exalted Christ. Verses 1, 4, and 9 include this emphasis. In fact, verse 9 says, *"I John,"* adding in the Greek word *ego* (for "I"). This indicates that John was emphatically drawing attention to himself. It's as if he was screaming to his readers, "Hey, it's me — John. *It's really me!*" Many believers across the Roman Empire were suffering for their faith at the time of John's writing, so this strong emphasis on his identity becomes even more important to his immediate family of readers.

John was the last living survivor of the original 12 apostles. Therefore, his letter to believers carried great weight and authority. When Christians heard that John was still alive, it was great news. Again and again, John confirmed, "It's really me — John. If you've wondered if I was alive or not, I am still here!"

'I John, Your *Brother*'

In Revelation 1:9, John wrote, "I John, who also am your brother and companion in tribulation, and in the kingdom and patience of Jesus

Christ, was in the isle that is called Patmos, for the word of God, and for the testimony of Jesus Christ."

Notice, John did not call himself the "illustrious apostle of Jesus," "the last survivor of the original 12," or even, "the one whom Jesus loved." Instead, he said I am your "brother," which is the Greek word *adelphos*. It was *a medical term used to describe two or more who were born from the same womb.* The word *adelphos* was later used in a military sense to depict *brothers, or comrades, in battle.*

Essentially, John told the believers he was writing to, "We were born from the same womb of humanity — and we were birthed from the same spiritual womb of God. What you're feeling and experiencing, I'm feeling and experiencing." Likewise, John was also saying, "We are comrades in battle — fellow soldiers in this spiritual war." John humbled himself, placing himself on the same level with other believers. It was as if he jumped down into the same foxhole with other Christians and let them know, "You're not in this fight alone. I'm right here fighting alongside you."

These words must have been supernaturally strengthening to believers who were suffering.

'I John, Your *Companion*'

Next, John calls himself a "companion in tribulation." The word "companion" is the Greek word *sugkoinonos*. It means *a companion or joint-partner; two or more who mutually share the same place, principles, problems, tasks, or circumstances.*

By using the word "companion" (*sugkoinonos*), John was saying, "You and I are in this thing together. I'm your brother — I'm your comrade and fellow soldier in battle, and I am proud to be a joint-partner, slugging it out with the enemy. And we are not giving up!"

As a *companion* to other believers, John said, "I am mutually sharing the same experience with you. The ordeal you're going through, I'm going through." Then he described the type of partnership they were engaged in — a partnership involving *tribulation* (*see* Revelation 1:9).

'Your Companion in *Tribulation*'

The word "tribulation" is the Greek word *thlipsis*, and it describes *affliction*, *trouble*, or *great pressure*; *crushing, suffocating pressure*; *a horribly tight, life-threatening squeeze.* At that time, John and his fellow believers were under persecution instigated by the Roman Emperor Domitian. He was against the Christian faith and was regularly killing those who followed Christ.

John was a good man who served the Body of Christ his entire life. He had committed no crimes. Yet one day while he was living in Ephesus, he was arrested by Roman soldiers and transported to Rome to stand trial before the emperor. When Domitian ordered John to recant his faith, the apostle refused. The emperor then ordered that John be thrown into a vat of boiling oil — a method of torture Romans used with regularity. Surely this would kill the last of the original 12 apostles. But it *didn't.*

Early Christian writers tell us that when they threw in the hooks to drag up John's skeleton, he was still alive and unscathed. Domitian was so terrified by the sight of this man who had been miraculously spared, he ordered that John be exiled to the isle of Patmos.

Patmos was a horrible, barren place of punishment. It had almost no trees and a very limited supply of fresh water. With only the clothes on his back, John was left to fend for himself — daily scavenging the island for food and water. Once he found a suitable cave, he took up residence there, and that is the place where Christ would step in and reveal Himself to John. It is where John received and wrote *The Revelation of Jesus Christ.*

In writing, John told believers, "If you feel like you're alone in the hardships you're facing, I want you to know you're not. I'm your companion in tribulation (*thlipsis*). It's not just you who are going through a suffocating time of pressure. I'm going through it too."

The Picture of Patience

John continued his opening address to believers by calling himself a companion "in the kingdom and patience of Jesus"(v. 9). The word "patience" is the Greek term *hupomone*, and it means *to stay or abide; to remain in one's spot and one's position*; *to resolve to maintain territory gained.* In a military sense, the word "patience" pictures *soldiers ordered to maintain their positions, even in the face of opposition, and to defiantly stick it out regardless of pressures mounted against them.*

"Patience" is *staying power*, *"hang-in-there" power*; *the attitude that holds out, holds on, outlasts, perseveres, and hangs in there, never giving up; it refuses to surrender to obstacles, and turns down every opportunity to quit.* It pictures *one under a heavy load, but who refuses to bend, break, or surrender because he is convinced that the territory, promise, or principle under assault rightfully belongs to him.* A better translation of the word "patience" would be *endurance*, *stamina*, or *durability*.

The apostle John was communicating, "Even though I'm living in a cave on this wretched island, I'm not going to quit! I am experiencing the *patience* of Jesus Christ." John had been given the supernatural enduring power of Christ, and it was enabling him to remain faithful to God even in the midst of life-threatening pressure. Anyone who decides to remain faithful to Jesus can receive this same divine endowment of endurance — including you.

Experiencing the Unexpected

Where was John when he received *The Revelation of Jesus Christ*? He said he "was in the isle that is called Patmos..." (Revelation 1:9). This word "was" is the Greek word *ginomai*, and it means *to transition from one realm to another*. It indicates a sudden or surprising change — something unexpected that takes one off guard. Basically, John was saying, "I could have never anticipated the series of events that brought me here."

What was also unexpected was John's experience with Jesus. He not only "was" in the isle called Patmos, but verse 10 says he "was" also, "...in the Spirit on the Lord's day...." Again, the Greek word *ginomai* is used. In this case, John's unexpected sudden change was a transition from the physical realm to the realm of the spirit. It is not a reference to the Holy Spirit, but to the spirit realm itself.

John had been suddenly and unexpectedly abandoned by society, but he was not abandoned by Jesus. When he had reached a point of unimaginable desolation, Christ showed up with revelation! The Holy Spirit transitioned John into another dimension, pulling back the curtains and revealing the kingly majesty of Jesus.

This means that no matter where you are or what you are going through, you can transition into the realm of the spirit to one degree or another. There, the Holy Spirit can speak to you and tell you exactly what you need to know.

Ephesus Was the First

Jesus Himself instructed John that what he saw he was to "…write in a book, and send it unto the seven churches which are in Asia; unto Ephesus, and unto Smyrna, and unto Pergamos, and unto Thyatira, and unto Sardis, and unto Philadelphia, and unto Laodicea" (Revelation 1:11).

Of all the churches mentioned, *Ephesus was the first.* Jesus addressed Ephesus first, as it was the city that housed the biggest church in the entire region.

What did the Lord say to John in that vision, and how does it apply to you today? The answers are ahead.

STUDY QUESTIONS

Study to shew thyself approved unto God, a workman that needeth not to be ashamed, rightly dividing the word of truth.
— 2 Timothy 2:15

1. Carefully read the main text of this lesson found in Revelation 1:9-11. What is the Holy Spirit showing you personally in this passage?
2. Receiving revelation from God is life-giving! What are some things you can do to position yourself to gain insights from God? Read these passages and write what He reveals: John 8:31, 32; Psalm 25:12-14; and First Corinthians 2:9, 10. (Also consider John 14:26; 16:13-15; and Romans 8:26, 27.)
3. In the midst of troubling situations, we often think, *Can anything good come out of this?* God answers, "Yes, something good *can* come out of this!" Read Romans 8:17, 18; Second Corinthians 4:16-18 and James 1:2-4. Then identify the good things you can expect on the other side of hardships. (Also consider Hebrews 12:7-11 and Psalm 119:67.)

PRACTICAL APPLICATION

But be ye doers of the word, and not hearers only, deceiving your own selves.
— James 1:22

1. To receive a "revelation" from God is *to see something clearly that was once veiled or hidden*. It could be something about God's character, a principle from Scripture, wisdom concerning a particular situation, or your identity in Christ. Take a moment and describe a revelation that you have received from God's Spirit that has been life-changing. Who or what did God use to "pull back the curtains" and bring illumination? How has this revelation made an impact on you?
2. The apostle John was in his 90s and had been walking with God for decades when he received the revelation of Jesus Christ. This lets us know that no matter how long we've been walking with God, there is always something new the Holy Spirit wants to show us. In light of your current circumstances and experiences, pray and ask the Holy Spirit to give you a fresh revelation of Jesus. Be still and listen. What is He revealing to you?
3. John was a faithful follower of Jesus Christ, and he faced great tribulation (*thlipsis*). How does knowing what John went through, and the fact that the Holy Spirit was with him every step of the way, encourage you in your faith?

LESSON 2

TOPIC

What Is the Church?

SCRIPTURES

1. **Revelation 1:10, 11** — I was in the Spirit on the Lord's day, and heard behind me a great voice, as of a trumpet, saying, I am Alpha and Omega, the first and the last: and, What thou seest, write in a book, and send it unto the seven churches which are in Asia; unto Ephesus, and unto Smyrna, and unto Pergamos, and unto Thyatira, and unto Sardis, and unto Philadelphia, and unto Laodicea.
2. **Revelation 2:1-7** — Unto the angel of the church of Ephesus write; These things saith he that holdeth the seven stars in his right hand, who walketh in the midst of the seven golden candlesticks; I know thy works, and thy labour, and thy patience, and how thou canst not bear them which are evil: and thou hast tried them which say they

are apostles, and are not, and hast found them liars: And hast borne, and hast patience, and for my name's sake hast laboured, and hast not fainted. Nevertheless I have somewhat against thee, because thou hast left thy first love. Remember therefore from whence thou art fallen, and repent, and do the first works; or else I will come unto thee quickly, and will remove thy candlestick out of his place, except thou repent. But this thou hast, that thou hatest the deeds of the Nicolaitans, which I also hate. He that hath an ear, let him hear what the Spirit saith unto the churches; To him that overcometh will I give to eat of the tree of life, which is in the midst of the paradise of God.

3. **Hebrews 12:22** — But ye are come unto mount Sion, and unto the city of the living God, the heavenly Jerusalem, and to an innumerable company of angels.
4. **Ecclesiastes 8:4** — Where the word of a king is, there is power....

GREEK WORDS

1. "angel" — (*angelos*): a word that describes either a human messenger or an angel; one who is sent on a special mission; one who is dispatched to perform a specific assignment; often used to denote a delegate or dignitary; it can picture the role of a pastor; a messenger of God
2. "church" — (*ekklesia*): a called, separated, and prestigious assembly; used to denote a prestigious assembly of distinguished Athenian citizens who determined laws, debated public policy, formulated new policies, argued and ruled in judicial matters, elected the chief magistrates of the land, and decided who should be banished; to be selected from society and invited to join this assembly was a great honor; in the New Testament, it depicts the body of believers who have been called out, called forth, selected, and assembled to be God's representatives in every town, city, state or nation; it is a body called to make decisions that affect the atmosphere of a region
3. "Ephesus" — (*Ephesos*): Ephesus, a city in Asia Minor

SYNOPSIS

The apostle Paul ministered in the ancient city of Ephesus for about three years, and during that time, the church of Ephesus was established. It became the largest, most significant church of the First Century and remained that way for almost 2,000 years. It was quite a spectacle of God's power, and from that city, churches were planted all across the province of Asia.

When Paul had completed his work at the church of Ephesus, Timothy became the pastor there. Years later, the apostle John moved to the region and became the bishop overseeing all the churches and pastors in Asia. It was in Ephesus where John wrote his gospel account as well as the books of First, Second, and Third John. Indeed, Ephesus was a magnificent city from which God's grace was poured out and great doctrinal instruction was dispersed. Amidst its intense wickedness, sexual debauchery, and paganism, the Holy Spirit used it as an epicenter to shake the world for Jesus.

The emphasis of this lesson:

The "angel" of the church of Ephesus was a special human messenger, hand-picked by Christ to oversee and care for the people. The word "church" describes a prestigious group of believers who are called out and separated from the world to rule and reign with spiritual authority on the earth.

John Entered the Realm of the Spirit

When John received the revelation of Jesus on the isle of Patmos, the Lord had some very serious things to say to the church of Ephesus — things that have great relevance for us today.

In Revelation 1:10, John wrote, "I was in the Spirit on the Lord's day, and heard behind me a great voice, as of a trumpet." We learned in our last lesson that the word "was" is the Greek word *ginomai*, and it describes *a sudden or unexpected transitioning from one realm to another*. A *ginomai* is something that takes one by surprise. By using this word, John was saying, "I transitioned from one realm into another realm, and the things that happened to me were totally unexpected."

First, John was on the isle of Patmos — a barren place of punishment. He was living in a cave and foraging for his food and water daily. The series of events that brought him to Patmos and the conditions he experienced were unforeseen. Yet while he had been abandoned by others, he was not abandoned by Jesus. Suddenly and unexpectedly, John found himself "in the Spirit," which would better be translated *in the realm of the spirit*. He entered a spiritual dimension where he saw Jesus like he had never seen Him before.

Jesus then spoke directly to John declaring, "I am Alpha and Omega, the first and the last: and what thou seest, write in a book, and send it unto the seven churches which are in Asia; unto Ephesus, and unto Smyrna, and unto Pergamos, and unto Thyatira, and unto Sardis, and unto Philadelphia, and unto Laodicea" (Revelation 1:11).

There were seven primary churches in Asia — they were the biggest and most influential at the time. And at the top of the list was the church of Ephesus. It was the largest and most influential church in the region.

Who Was the *Angel* of the Church of Ephesus?

Jesus told John, "Unto the angel of the church of Ephesus write..." (Revelation 2:1). Who was this angel? Was it a supernatural being from Heaven, or was it someone else? The word "angel" is the Greek word *angelos*, and it describes either *a heavenly angel* or *a human messenger*. It is *one who is sent on a special mission*; *one dispatched to perform a specific assignment*. It is often used to denote *a delegate* or *dignitary*.

In Rick's book *A Light in Darkness, Volume One*, he clearly delineates what "angel" means in Revelation 2:1. He writes:

> Although local churches may have angels that watch over and protect them, it is unlikely that the word "angel" here refers to heavenly messengers.... Jesus was addressing the human messengers of the seven churches, the individuals — most notably the pastors — who had oversights of the congregations. These messengers were the pastors of the seven churches.

It is important to note that there is not a single instance recorded in the New Testament in which angels teach or preach to the Church of Jesus Christ. Neither do they rebuke or bring correction to its members. To say that a heavenly being is being referred to in Revelation 2 would create serious theological inconsistencies.

In this passage, Jesus was addressing the seven *pastors* who were overseeing the local churches, not heavenly angels. By delivering His messages to the pastors first, Jesus demonstrated that He honors and does not bypass the spiritual authority He has established in the Church.

Once the pastors heard the message from Jesus, it was their responsibility to deliver it to the people under those pastors' care. Pastors are Heaven-sent messengers who speak on behalf of the Lord. The Lord speaks to them first. They then have the responsibility to process the message and pass it on to the congregation.

What Do Angels Do?

Although the Bible doesn't explicitly reveal how many angels God created, it does say in Hebrews 12:22 that there are "…an innumerable company of angels" in the Church. Angels meet physical needs, give supernatural strength and guidance, provide protection and deliverance, and perform superhuman feats. They also worship God and release His judgment on the earth. Angels are also known for making divine announcements. These assignments are all well documented throughout the pages of the Old and New Testaments.

It's important to note again that there is no record in the New Testament that endorses the concept of angels being given the responsibility of preaching or teaching God's Word. There is not one instance in which God sent an angel to bring correction or rebuke to a local congregation of believers. Although angels have delivered divine announcements, they only *repeat* verbatim what God says — no more, no less.

The apostle Paul strongly warned against a preoccupation with angels (*see* Galatians 1:8, 9). The doctrinal problems that he combated during the First Century were linked with revelations that supposedly came directly from angels. Such was the case with the church of Colossae. So-called angelic preaching and teaching was viewed as a primary source of false doctrine in the Early Church. It is no surprise that many cults and sects that exist today were also formed on the basis of alleged angelic or "otherworldly" revelations and teachings.

To be clear, the fivefold ministry gifts, which include preaching and teaching the Word, were entrusted to humans, not angels. If anyone tells you he has a revelation or teaching that he received from an angel — and it contradicts God's Word — you should reject that message.

What Does the Word 'Church' Really Mean?

Jesus told John, "Unto the angel [which we now know is the pastor] of the church of Ephesus write…" (Revelation 2:1). Notice the word "church." When you hear that word, what usually comes to mind? What do you think early New Testament believers thought of when they heard the word "church"?

The word "church" comes from the Greek word *ekklesia*, and it signifies *a called, separated, and very prestigious assembly*. Originally, it was used to denote a prestigious assembly of distinguished Athenian citizens who determined laws, debated public policy, formulated new policies, argued and ruled in judicial matters, elected the chief magistrates of the land, and decided who should be banished. To be selected from society to join this assembly by invitation was a great honor.

Ekklesia is a compound of two words — *ek* and *kaleo*. *Ek* primarily means *out*, and it can signify an *exit*, such as when a person leaves one room to relocate to another room. The word *kaleo* means *to beckon*, *to call*, *to invite*, or *to summon*. When *ek* and *kaleo* are compounded, the new word *ekklesia* literally means *those that are called out*. *Ekklesia* describes an entire assembly of individuals who are called out, called forth, separated, and who hold a position of honor and privilege.

In the New Testament, the word "church" (*ekklesia*) depicts the body of believers who have been called out, called forth, selected, and assembled to be God's representatives in every town, city, state, or nation. The local church is a body called to make decisions that affect the atmosphere of a region.

An Honor and a Privilege

Paul and the New Testament writers clearly understood the depth of meaning of the word *ekklesia*. It was no accident that they selected this word to depict the local church and its role in God's plan. The Athenian *ekklesia*, which early believers were well acquainted with, was considered the most prestigious group of people in the land. It was a renowned institution throughout the entire Greek-speaking world. People counted it a great privilege and honor to participate in this illustrious body.

We are honored and privileged to be called out to be a member of Jesus' Church. As the Church of the Lord Jesus Christ, we are a prestigious people who have been called out of darkness, called out of a life of sin, and endowed with great authority and power so that we can make the ruling decisions of the land.

The Church was not meant to be a little fringe group of people that hides in a corner. Through prayer, preaching and teaching, godly lifestyles, and a proactive stance against the world's evil practices, the Early Church had the ability to affect the atmosphere of a city or nation in which they lived — and we still do as the Church today! We are meant to be God's ruling force *in every place* we are positioned on earth. This is the Church!

STUDY QUESTIONS

Study to shew thyself approved unto God, a workman that needeth not to be ashamed, rightly dividing the word of truth.
— 2 Timothy 2:15

1. The Bible has much to say about angels, and as a child of God, it is good for you to know how He has assigned them to help you. Read Hebrews 1:14; Psalm 91:11, 12; Luke 22:43; and Acts 12:6-10. Identify some of the ways in which angels assist us on earth. How do these verses encourage you?
2. Humans, not angels, are given the responsibility and privilege to preach and teach the Word of God. Read Ephesians 4:11-14 and name the fivefold ministry gifts Christ has given to the Church. Include the overall purpose for their service to the Body of Christ.
3. As a member of the Church of the Lord Jesus Christ, you are a part of a prestigious people! Write down what the Holy Spirit reveals to you from the following passages about being a member of Christ's Church: 1 Peter 2:9-11; Ephesians 1:4, 5; 1 John 3:1-3; 1 Corinthians 1:26-31.

PRACTICAL APPLICATION

But be ye doers of the word, and not hearers only, deceiving your own selves.
— James 1:22

1. When you hear the word "church," what do you think of? Describe your thoughts.
2. Carefully review the definition of *ekklesia* — the Greek word for "church." How does the meaning of this word expand your understanding of what God has called you to be a part of?
3. God has strategically placed your pastor in the place of leadership in your church. He is like an *angel* — hand-picked as Heaven's messenger to help you and those around you grow and mature in your faith. After receiving this insight, what adjustments do you sense the Holy Spirit is asking you to make in your attitude toward your pastor and his family?

LESSON 3

TOPIC

Why Stars in Christ's Right Hand?

SCRIPTURES

1. **2 Timothy 1:7** — For God hath not given us the spirit of fear; but of power, and of love, and of a sound mind.
2. **Revelation 1:9-11** — I John, who also am your brother, and companion in tribulation, and in the kingdom and patience of Jesus Christ, was in the isle that is called Patmos, for the word of God, and for the testimony of Jesus Christ. I was in the Spirit on the Lord's day, and heard behind me a great voice, as of a trumpet, saying, I am Alpha and Omega, the first and the last: and, What thou seest, write in a book, and send it unto the seven churches which are in Asia; unto Ephesus, and unto Smyrna, and unto Pergamos, and unto Thyatira, and unto Sardis, and unto Philadelphia, and unto Laodicea.
3. **Revelation 2:1** — Unto the angel of the church of Ephesus write; These things saith he that holdeth the seven stars in his right hand, who walketh in the midst of the seven golden candlesticks.

GREEK WORDS

1. "church" — (*ekklesia*): a called, separated, and prestigious assembly; used to denote a prestigious assembly of distinguished Athenian citizens who determined laws, debated public policy, formulated new policies, argued and ruled in judicial matters, elected the chief magistrates of the land, and decided who should be banished; to be selected from society and invited to join this assembly was a great honor; in the New Testament, it depicts the body of believers who have been called out, called forth, selected, and assembled to be God's representatives in every town, city, state, or nation; a body called to make decisions that affect the atmosphere of a region
2. "walketh" — ϖ ϖ (*peripateo*): to walk around; to live and carry on in one general vicinity; pictures a person who has walked on one path or vicinity for so long that he can now almost walk that path blindfolded; this person knows this path because he has habitually

lived and functioned there; denotes the movement of the feet; it suggests one who has walked in one region for so long that it has now become his environment, his place of daily activity; often translated to live or to stroll

3. "midst"— μ (*mesos*): right in the very center; in the very midst; to be in the gut or heart of a thing
4. "golden"— (*chrusos*): gold; the most valuable material that existed in the ancient world; it denotes that which is rare and highly prized; can be used figuratively to denote something precious or of great significance
5. "candlesticks"— (*luchnia*): an oil-burning lamp carried by hand, positioned on a table or elevated on a stand; such lamps were fashioned of earthen clay with a reservoir to hold oil and a wick that gave light in darkness once it was lighted; oil-burning lamps were vital to life because they were the only source of light in the darkness
6. "holdeth"— (*krateo*): a masterful grip; to tightly embrace; to hold fast
7. "stars"— (*asteros*): plural form of the word "star"; the word to describe the stars in the universe

SYNOPSIS

Curetes Street is one of the oldest and most illustrious streets in the ancient city of Ephesus. A person walking this avenue more than 2,000 years ago would have seen beautiful covered colonnades that lined the street on each side, as well as detailed mosaic floors. Colorful statues of poets, educators, politicians, governors, and prestigious citizens were also visible along this road. And Curetes Street led to the library and synagogue that were once located in the very heart of the city.

This street was the place from which the Gospel "exploded" and went out to all of Asia. It was on this very street that Timothy, the pastor of the Ephesian church, once walked. As historians tell it, Timothy came out one day to confront those participating in a pagan parade that had traveled this route in celebration of idolatry. The people responded to his rebuke by beating him on the spot. Some believe that Timothy died as a martyr on Curetes Street at the age of 80.

Earlier in Timothy's life, he battled with a spirit of fear. The apostle Paul, who served as the younger minister's mentor, had written to him, "For God hath not given us the spirit of fear; but of power, and of love, and of a sound mind" (2 Timothy 1:7). Clearly, to boldly denounce the ungodly acts of those people to their face, Timothy must have overcome that spirit of fear. And if *you* are battling a spirit of fear, God will help you overcome too.

The emphasis of this lesson:

In the midst of unforeseen, unexpected events, John found himself transported to the realm of the spirit, where he received a powerful revelation of Christ. From part of that vision, we can ascertain that Jesus masterfully holds the pastors of His Church in His mighty grip. *Nothing* and *no one* can remove them from His hand. Jesus not only calls them "angels," but also "stars" that shine in the darkness of this world. Jesus is permanently walking in the midst of His Church, including local church congregations across the world.

'In the Isle That Is Called Patmos'

Just before John began to unfold the revelation of Jesus, he said, "I John, who also am your brother, and companion in tribulation, and in the kingdom and patience of Jesus Christ, was in the isle that is called Patmos, for the word of God, and for the testimony of Jesus Christ" (Revelation 1:9). As we have seen, the word "was" is the Greek word *ginomai*. By using this word, John was saying, in effect, "I could have never anticipated the series of events that brought me here."

Everyone knew the name "Patmos" and the dreadful stigma attached to that place. It was a forbidden, forsaken island, stripped of nearly all foliage. Virtually nothing but barren rock and a single source of fresh water could be found there at the time of John's exile.

Being a political prisoner, John was deposited on the island with nothing more than the clothes on his back. He was not incarcerated in a prison cell, but was left to roam the island and to scavenge for food and water. In his 90s, the apostle was reduced to living in a cave — a cave one can still visit, which today is called the Cave of the Revelation.

'In the Spirit on the Lord's Day'

John then wrote, "I was in the Spirit on the Lord's day, and heard behind me a great voice, as of a trumpet" (Revelation 1:10). In the *King James Version*, the word "Spirit" is capitalized. However, in the original Greek writing, it is not. This word does not refer to the Holy Spirit, but instead to *a spiritual dimension*.

Again, John used the word "was," which is the Greek word *ginomai*. Here, it describes *an unexpected, unanticipated transition from one realm to another realm*. So when John says, "I was in the spirit," it could be taken to mean, "Somehow, I found myself transitioning from the physical realm to a spiritual dimension." When he was in that spiritual dimension, he received the revelation of Jesus Christ and all that is contained in the pages of what we now call the book of Revelation.

All of this happened "on the Lord's day." The phrase "Lord's day" does not refer to the Sabbath day or to Sunday. It is the Greek term *kuriakos*, which is the word for *the Imperial Day of the Emperor*. This was the day on which Domitian, the emperor of Rome, was worshiped across the entire empire. Essentially, John was saying, "When the rest of the Roman world was worshiping the pagan Emperor Domitian, *on that very day*, Jesus Christ the Eternal Emperor stepped into my cave and gave me this revelation."

Ephesus Was First

In Revelation 1:11, Jesus named seven specific churches with which John was to share this message: "Unto Ephesus, unto Smyrna, unto Pergamum, unto Thyatira, unto Sardis, unto Philadelphia, and unto Laodicea." The first church listed was the Church of Ephesus.

Ephesus was listed first because it was the first church birthed in all of Asia. It was also the largest, *most notable*, *most powerful*, and *most influential* church in the entire region. Furthermore, Ephesus was considered the "light of Asia." That is, it was believed that whatever happened in Ephesus would eventually affect the entire Asian continent. From Ephesus, roads spread outward to all other major cities and brought with them the philosophy, education, and culture of this illustrious city.

Jesus was and is very strategic in everything He does. The Gospel first came to Ephesus so that it, too, could be taken "on many roads" to the whole province of Asia.

The *Angel* of the *Church*

Christ told John to give the message to "the angel of the church of Ephesus." In our last lesson, we learned that the word "angel" is the Greek word *angelos*. Although this word can refer to heavenly angels, in this verse, it specifically describes *a human messenger*, not a heavenly being. Specifically, this word referred to *the pastor of the church*.

It's important to see that when Christ had something to say to the local church, He honored the spiritual authority that He had established. He didn't address the church directly; He addressed the pastor of the church first. And if Christ has a message of correction or rebuke He needs to speak to a church today, He will speak to the pastor first. It is then the pastor's responsibility to process the message and transmit it to the congregation he oversees.

Jesus said, "Unto the *pastor* of the *church* write...." The word "church" is the Greek word *ekklesia*, and it is the compound of two words: *ek*, meaning *out*, and *kaleo*, meaning *to call* or *to summon*. When *ek* and *kaleo* are compounded, they form the word *ekklesia*, meaning *someone who makes an exit from society and is called to something different*.

Historically, the word *ekklesia* denoted *a prestigious public assembly of distinguished Athenian citizens who were selected and called out of society*. It was most notably used to describe this group of people who gathered about 40 times per year to determine laws, debate public policy, formulate new policies, and argue judicial cases. The Athenian *ekklesia* elected the chief magistrates of the land. They were a group of people who were greatly honored.

In the New Testament, *ekklesia* is used to depict the prestigious body of believers who have been called out of the world and separated unto Christ to be God's representatives in every town, city, state, and nation. The Church is a body called to make decisions that affect the atmosphere of the region where they live. It is not just a small building on a street corner, nor is it a group of people meant to hide from the rest of the world. As the Church — the *ekklesia* — we are called to be God's ruling voice in the town, city, state, or nation where we are located.

The 'Stars in His Right Hand'

Jesus continued speaking to John in Revelation 2:1, saying, "...These things saith he that holdeth the seven stars in his right hand, who walketh in the midst of the seven golden candlesticks."

In Christ's right hand were "seven stars." These stars represent the seven pastors of the seven churches in Asia. Interestingly, the pastors are called *angels* and *stars*. The word "stars" is the Greek word *asteros*, and it describes *the stars in the universe*. By using this word, Jesus was saying that the pastors were to *shine like stars in the spiritual darkness that permeated the region.* They were to be guiding lights to the people within their congregations. They were to help navigate the lost toward Christ, assist believers in worship, and teach the Word in such a way that people could grasp it.

Like the stars in the heavens, each pastor's ministry is temporary. There is no such thing as a permanent pastor. Eventually, the time will come when his light will begin to fade, and a new star will be born to take his place. The lifespan of a pastor's ministry is dependent on a number of factors. The amount of spiritual fuel he has at his core is key, which is also true of natural stars.

Very often, pastors of larger churches have shorter ministries because they experience such great pressure at their core, causing them to utilize more spiritual fuel and burn out more quickly. Pastors of smaller churches may not shine as brightly in regard to prominence or fame, but they tend to shine their light longer as they experience less pressure at their core.

The amount of spiritual fuel resident in a pastor, his use of that fuel, and his ability to endure pressure at his core are all critical factors that determine the longevity of his ministry. Just as no two stars are exactly alike, pastors are also individually very unique. While some are called to lead small churches, others are called to lead medium- or large-sized churches. Yet all pastors are important and valuable in God's plan. Jesus calls them *stars* and *angels*, and we should treat them with the honor and respect they deserve.

In the Grip of Greatness

The seven stars, or *pastors*, addressed in the book of Revelation were being held by Christ. Revelation 2:1 says He "holdeth" them in His right hand. The word "holdeth" is the Greek word *kratos* — a word that denotes great power. It describes *a masterful grip*. It means *to tightly embrace or to hold fast whatever is being held*. Here, it depicts Jesus tightly holding and embracing these pastors — gripping them so strongly that no one could take them from Him. They were totally in His control. Jesus is the Great Shepherd, and pastors are the under-shepherds. Pastors are expected to deliver with accuracy Jesus' message to their respective congregations.

Notice these pastors were not in the hands of a board of deacons or a pulpit committee. Although these kinds of groups provide accountability and have purpose, each pastor is called by Jesus and is first and foremost answerable to Him. Christ powerfully and masterfully holds each pastor in His mighty grip.

Christ 'Walketh in the Midst' of the Church

In Revelation 2, the churches that were specifically addressed were the seven most influential congregations in Asia at that time. But we can be certain that Christ's messages to those churches should be heeded as admonitions and encouragement to His Church today.

As Jesus held the seven stars, or pastors, in His right hand, the Scripture says He "...walketh in the midst of the seven golden candlesticks" (Revelation 2:1). The word "walketh" is the Greek word *peripateo*. It means to *walk around, live, and carry on in one general vicinity*. It pictures a person who has walked on one path for so long that he can now almost walk that path blindfolded. This person knows the path because he has habitually functioned there. The word *peripateo* denotes the movement of the feet of one who has walked in one region for so long that it has now become his environment, his place of daily activity. It is also translated *to stroll*.

In this verse, we find Christ in a place where He was perpetually walking in the midst of those seven golden "candlesticks"— those influential churches in that province of Asia. And among His churches is the vicinity where Jesus still walks and operates today. Jesus is constantly moving His feet — *peripateo* — and walking among His churches.

Of course, God is omniscient and omnipresent, but Christ's birds-eye view of those churches in the book of Revelation was key in His addressing their specific problems with such accuracy. The church of Ephesus was one of great power and influence. But it was not a congregation without issues. However, Jesus addressed those problems, and what He spoke to them, He is still speaking today.

STUDY QUESTIONS

Study to shew thyself approved unto God, a workman that needeth not to be ashamed, rightly dividing the word of truth.
— 2 Timothy 2:15

1. Timothy battled a spirit of fear earlier in his life, but God helped him overcome it. Are you fighting against fear? God wants to bring you peace and confidence just like He did for Timothy. Read Isaiah 41:10-13; Psalm 27:1-5; Psalm 91; and Hebrews 13:5, 6. Then take a few minutes to mediate on these promises, and write out one (or more) verse that especially encourages you and brings you peace.
2. Before this lesson, what was your understanding of the *seven stars* held by Christ in the book of Revelation? How about the words "holdeth" and "walketh"? How has your understanding of the stars and Jesus' interaction with them changed?

PRACTICAL APPLICATION

But be ye doers of the word, and not hearers only, deceiving your own selves.
— James 1:22

1. The apostle John "was" (*ginomai*) on the isle of Patmos. That is, he found himself in a situation that was totally unexpected and unforeseen — and even undesirable. Have you ever been in such a situation? Are you in one now? Take a moment and describe the challenge you currently face.
2. In the midst of the series of unanticipated events that landed John on the forsaken, desolate island of Patmos, he received a life-changing revelation of Christ! When he least expected it, he transitioned into another spiritual dimension and saw Jesus as he had never seen Him before. How does this spark hope in you in the midst of what *you're* facing?

LESSON 4

TOPIC

Why Candlesticks?

SCRIPTURES

1. **Revelation 1:10-13** — I was in the Spirit on the Lord's day, and heard behind me a great voice, as of a trumpet, saying, I am Alpha and Omega, the first and the last: and, What thou seest, write in a book, and send it unto the seven churches which are in Asia; unto Ephesus, and unto Smyrna, and unto Pergamos, and unto Thyatira, and unto Sardis, and unto Philadelphia, and unto Laodicea. And I turned to see the voice that spake with me. And being turned, I saw seven golden candlesticks; and in the midst of the seven candlesticks one like unto the Son of man, clothed with a garment down to the foot, and girt about the paps with a golden girdle.
2. **Revelation 2:1-3** — Unto the angel of the church of Ephesus write; these things saith he that holdeth the seven stars in his right hand, who walketh in the midst of the seven golden candlesticks; I know thy works, and thy labour, and thy patience, and how thou canst not bear them which are evil: and thou hast tried them which say they are apostles, and are not, and hast found them liars: And hast borne, and hast patience, and for my name's sake hast laboured, and hast not fainted.

GREEK WORDS

1. "walketh" — ϖ ϖ (*peripateo*): to walk around; to live and carry on in one general vicinity; the picture of a person who has walked on one path or vicinity for so long that he can almost walk that path blindfolded; this person knows this path because he has habitually lived and functioned there; denotes the movement of the feet; it suggests one who has walked in one region for so long that it has now become his environment, his place of daily activity; often translated to live or to stroll
2. "midst" — **μ** (*mesos*): right in the very center; in the very midst; to be in the gut or heart of a thing

3. "golden" — (*chrusos*): gold; the most valuable material that existed in the ancient world; it denotes that which is rare and highly prized; can be used figuratively to denote something precious or of great significance
4. "candlesticks" — (*luchnia*): an oil-burning lamp carried by hand, positioned on a table or elevated on a stand; such lamps were fashioned of earthen clay with a reservoir to hold oil and a wick that gave light in darkness once it was lighted; oil-burning lamps were vital to life because they were the only source of light in darkness

SYNOPSIS

In approximately 52 BC, the apostle Paul and his ministry team members, Aquila and Priscilla, had completed their work in the city of Corinth. The church of Corinth was firmly established, and it was time for them to move on to the next place where God would lead them. They boarded a ship in Cenchreae, a port in Greece, and sailed across the Aegean Sea to the city of Ephesus.

At that time, there were no believers present in the pagan city of Ephesus. It was a very dark environment filled with all kinds of idolatry and sexual debauchery. Paul and his companions went right to the heart of the city and began to preach the Word. Apollos was one of the first people they met and led to the Lord. God was with Paul and his team, as evidenced by many special miracles, signs, and wonders that He performed through them.

Within a short time, the mighty church of Ephesus was birthed, and God continued to liberally pour out His grace among the people. Before long, what was happening in Ephesus began to move out and impact the entire region of Asia. Indeed, the church of Ephesus was an amazing center of God's glory. Yet it was not without problems. Christ brought correction, along with praise, to this body of believers, as we will see.

The emphasis of this lesson:

Jesus Christ is holding His Church tightly within His right hand. He loves the Church and permanently lives in the heart of each of His people. In spite of our failures and flaws, Christ views the Church as rare, priceless gold. We were made to be filled with the oil of His Spirit and to burn brightly and uniquely wherever He chooses to place us.

What We've Learned So Far

The apostle John "was" on the isle of Patmos. "Was" is the Greek word *ginomai*, and it means *to transition from one realm to another*. It indicates *something unexpected that takes one off guard*. Through a series of unforeseen events, John was banished to the island of Patmos. He was left to fend for himself and ended up living in a cave there for about 18 months.

John related a spectacular experience he had in that cave one day, saying, "I was in the Spirit on the Lord's day, and heard behind me a great voice, as of a trumpet" (Revelation 1:10). Again, the word "was" is the Greek word *ginomai*. Essentially, John was saying, "Something happened that completely took me by surprise. Suddenly, I found myself transitioning from the physical realm to the realm of the spirit." It was in this dimension of the spirit that John received his revelation of Jesus Christ.

The voice John heard was the voice of Christ, "Saying, I am Alpha and Omega, the first and the last: and, what thou seest, write in a book and send it unto the seven churches which are in Asia; unto Ephesus, and unto Smyrna, and unto Pergamos, and unto Thyatira, and unto Sardis, and unto Philadelphia, and unto Laodicea" (Revelation 1:11). Jesus spoke with a sense of urgency. "Write this, and write it now," He urged. "And send it to the seven churches in Asia."

Ephesus was the first church Christ addressed. It was the first church established and it was the largest and most influential church in the region. By addressing Ephesus first, Christ set in motion a message that would eventually reach all of the seven churches in that ancient province.

Jesus said, "Unto the angel of the church of Ephesus write; these things saith he that holdeth the seven stars in his right hand, who walketh in the midst of the seven golden candlesticks" (Revelation 2:1).

'Angel' — *Angelos*

We discovered that the word "angel" is the Greek word *angelos*, which refers to *the messenger*, *the overseer*, or *the pastor* of the church.

'Church' — *Ekklesia*

The word "church" is the Greek word *ekklesia*. It is taken from the words *ek* and *kaleo*. *Ek* means *out*, and it is where we get the word *exit*. *Kaleo* means *to call or summon*. When these words are put together, they form *ekklesia*, which is a term borrowed from the Athenian culture.

In Athens, there was an *ekklesia* — a political body of people who were called out from society to rule and reign and make decisions regarding public policies and more. The apostle Paul and the other writers of the New Testament understood the meaning of the word *ekklesia* and selected it for our word "church." It was no accident that this word was chosen.

The "church" — the *ekklesia* of the New Testament — is made up of people *who have been called to make an exit from society in order to rule and reign in the decisions made in our towns, cities, states, and nations*. As the Church, we have been called out, separated, and summoned to a prestigious body of believers that are to be God's dominating voice in every place we live.

'Holdeth' — *Kratos*

Jesus "holdeth the seven stars in his right hand…" (Revelation 2:1). "Holdeth" is derived from the Greek word *kratos*, which describes *a very powerful grip*. The seven stars are the seven pastors *being masterfully held* in Christ's right hand. The right hand always symbolizes *ruling power*. The pastors of the seven churches were not in the hands of a deacon board or pulpit committee. They were securely held in the right hand of Jesus Himself.

Like stars, pastors are called to shine and serve as guiding lights in the darkness for their congregations and communities. They provide direction and the illumination of truth. Pastors are accountable and answerable first and foremost to Christ.

'Walketh' — *Peripateo*

Jesus "…walketh in the midst of the seven golden candlesticks" (Revelation 2:1). The word "walketh" is the Greek word *peripateo*, and it means *to walk around* or *to live and carry on in one general vicinity*. It is the picture of a person who has walked on one path so long that he can almost walk the path blindfolded. This person knows the path like the back of his hand. He has habitually functioned there, and it has become the environment in which he lives and strolls.

Who was doing the walking? Jesus. *Where* was He walking and functioning? In the midst of the seven churches. The Church is where Jesus habitually lives. It is His place of residence. He knows it intimately and loves it.

Jesus gave His life for the Church. Therefore, He is in constant connection with His Church.

John said in Revelation 1:12 and 13, "And I turned to see the voice that spake with me. And being turned, I saw seven golden candlesticks; and in the midst of the seven candlesticks one like unto the Son of man, clothed with a garment down to the foot, and girt about the paps with a golden girdle."

In Christ's Eyes, We're Golden — and He Is in Our Midst!

The seven golden candlesticks represent the seven churches in Asia (*see* Revelation 1:20). The "One" in the midst of those seven churches was Jesus. The word "midst" here and in Revelation 2:1 is the Greek word *mesos*, which means *right in the very center, in the gut, or heart of a thing*. Christ, the Son of Man, was right in the heart of the Church! He is habitually and actively connected with His *ekklesia* — His prestigious body of called-out ones who represent His ruling authority on the earth.

The word "golden" is the Greek word *chrusos*, meaning *gold — the most valuable metal that existed in the ancient world*. Gold denotes *that which is rare and highly prized*. It can be used figuratively to denote something precious or of great significance.

Ironically, when we read Christ's words to the seven churches, He exposes a number of problems they had. Although it may appear that most of these churches were defective in some way, that is not the way Christ saw them. He said they were "golden." In other words, when He looks at the Church, it is very precious and rare to Him; nothing is more valuable. He shed His blood and gave His life for the Church. He was raised to new life and now sits at the right hand of the Father, ever interceding for the Church.

Jesus' view of the Church should be *our* view of the Church. Yes, the Church has problems. The seven churches in the book of Revelation had problems too. In fact, five of them received a serious rebuke from Jesus. However, in His eyes they were still golden, and His Church today is golden too.

Why Candlesticks?

Jesus called the seven churches "candlesticks." This is the Greek word *luchnia*. It describes *oil-burning lamps carried by hand, positioned on a table or elevated on a stand*. Such lamps were fashioned of earthen clay and had a reservoir to hold oil and a wick that gave light in darkness once it was lighted. Oil-burning lamps were vital to early New Testament life because they were the only source of light in the darkness.

The candlesticks John had in mind when he penned these words were nothing like what most people might envision. They were not baton-shaped and made out of wax with a wick running through the center. Candlesticks like these were not invented until approximately 1,000 years after these words were written. The kind of candlesticks Christ referred to were oil-burning lamps that were handmade from clay and were very fragile. They were so fragile that they could easily be broken by merely squeezing them in one's hand.

Symbolically, each church — and each believer for that matter — is like one of these oil-burning lamps. The Church is made up of fragile, imperfect human beings. But God has chosen the Church as His primary instrument for giving light to the dark world around us.

Just as each clay lamp contained oil as its fuel, each church and each believer contains the "oil" of the Holy Spirit. Although the Church and the people who make it up have many weaknesses, God has graciously chosen to deposit the oil of His Holy Spirit inside us to extend His life-giving light to the very ends of the earth.

In order for the oil in those clay lamps to burn and produce light, a wick was required. The wick was inserted into the mouth of the lamp, and it ran deep into the lamp's reservoir where the oil resided. Being saturated with the oil, the end of the wick in the mouth of the lamp could be ignited, and it would burn and provide light for hours.

In the same way, the Church (and each individual believer) has a reservoir to contain the Holy Spirit's oil. How do we as the Church give off light? Just as the fiery light of the lamp was in the lamp's mouth, the outlet for the Holy Spirit's fire is the believer's mouth. It burns and gives light through the preaching, teaching, and proclaiming of God's Word.

No Two Lamps Were Alike

An interesting fact about these oil-burning lamps is that no two were exactly alike. Being handmade, they all had slightly different shapes and unique patterns and characteristics. In the same way, there are no two churches exactly alike — neither are any two believers identical.

You should never try to be exactly like another believer. You should strive to be who God created *you* to be. Likewise, no church should try to duplicate another church. Each church should have its own unique characteristics and fill its specific niche in the Body of Christ.

One last note of importance is the lamp's handle. In order for a lamp to be transported from one place to another, a person would take it by the handle and direct its light where he needed it.

In the same way, each church and each believer is in the hand of Christ. He has the right and authority to direct each one as He pleases. We are His light in the darkness; we are not our own.

STUDY QUESTIONS

Study to shew thyself approved unto God, a workman that needeth not to be ashamed, rightly dividing the word of truth.
— 2 Timothy 2:15

1. When Christ spoke to the seven churches of Asia, He pointed out some things that really needed to change in them. Yet in His eyes, they were still viewed as priceless *gold*. Be honest: How do you think Jesus sees you? Read these promises from His Word: 2 Corinthians 5:17, 21; Acts 13:38, 39; 1 John 3:1, 2; Romans 8:16, 17; and Galatians 4:7. Now describe how He really sees you — and how He wants you to see yourself.
2. Just as each of the seven churches was an oil-burning lamp meant to give off light, you, too, are meant to burn brightly for God's glory. But you need the "oil" of His Spirit for fuel. How important is the oil, and how do you acquire this priceless commodity? (Consider Zechariah 4:6; Micah 3:8; Acts 1:8; Ephesians 5:18; 1 Corinthians 14:4; Jude 1:20.)

PRACTICAL APPLICATION

But be ye doers of the word, and not hearers only, deceiving your own selves.
—James 1:22

1. In this lesson, we learned that Jesus sees each of us as an oil-burning lamp. We each have unique characteristics and a purpose that is all our own. Be honest: Are you aspiring to be like another believer you admire? If so, who? What do you appreciate most about that person?
2. What is it about *you* that makes you unique and different from other believers? What do others appreciate about you that you, too, can learn to celebrate? (Think about things others have sought your help with or complimented you about through the years.)

LESSON 5

TOPIC

Doctrinal Integrity

SCRIPTURES

1. **1 Timothy 4:1** — Now the Spirit speaketh expressly, that in the latter times some shall depart from the faith, giving heed to seducing spirits, and doctrines of devils.
2. **Revelation 1:10-13** — I was in the Spirit on the Lord's day, and heard behind me a great voice, as of a trumpet, saying, I am Alpha and Omega, the first and the last: and, what thou seest, write in a book, and send it unto the seven churches which are in Asia; unto Ephesus, and unto Smyrna, and unto Pergamos, and unto Thyatira, and unto Sardis, and unto Philadelphia, and unto Laodicea. And I turned to see the voice that spake with me. And being turned, I saw seven golden candlesticks; and in the midst of the seven candlesticks one like unto the Son of man, clothed with a garment down to the foot, and girt about the paps with a golden girdle.
3. **Revelation 2:1, 2** — Unto the angel of the church of Ephesus write; these things saith he that holdeth the seven stars in his right hand, who walketh in the midst of the seven golden candlesticks; I know

thy works, and thy labour, and thy patience, and how thou canst not bear them which are evil: and thou hast tried them which say they are apostles, and are not, and hast found them liars.

GREEK WORDS

1. "know" — (*oida*): to see; to behold; to perceive; to delightfully view; pictures a scrutinizing look; to look with the intent to examine; to fully view; to experience; to know from personal observation
2. "works" — (*erga*): some kind of action, deed, or activity; referred to a person's occupation, labor, or things produced by someone's effort or life; denoted the result of hard work or hard labor; pictures a person's line of work, career, or profession; this word is so all-encompassing that it also pictures actions, beliefs, and conduct

SYNOPSIS

Nearly major city in the Roman Empire had a *bouleuterion.* The word *bouleuterion* means *the place of counselors.* The *bouleuterion* was the location where leaders of communities met and discussed the issues of the day. It was, in effect, a city council, where high-ranking individuals talked about taxation and laws in the public sector, as well as private affairs, such as how to resolve societal problems and confront other key issues that challenged society. The First Century was a very dark time in history riddled with all kinds of problems that affected every sector of life.

There is nothing new under the sun. In our society today, we're experiencing problems on every front where spiritual darkness has been allowed to run rampant and reign. The apostle Paul said, "...The Spirit speaketh expressly, that in the latter times some shall depart from the faith, giving heed to seducing spirits, and doctrines of devils" (1 Timothy 4:1). The word "expressly" is the Greek word *rhetos*, which means the Spirit was speaking *emphatically, clearly, and unmistakably — leaving no room for doubt.* What did the Spirit say? He said that at the end of the age, just before Christ returns, demonic spirits will run rampantly throughout the world, leading people astray and causing innumerable problems.

We are living at the end of the age — at the very time to which the Holy Spirit was referring. The good news is, we don't have to be a victim of the times. We can overcome life's challenges through the power of God's Word, the power of the Holy Spirit, and the power of Jesus' shed blood.

We have been ordained by God to live victoriously for Christ in *any* age or season — even in the darkest of times — and He has certainly chosen us to be alive on this planet at this marker in time.

The emphasis of this lesson:

Just as there were problems in the First-Century Church, there are problems in the Church today. Yet in spite of our issues, Jesus sees us as *precious*, *priceless* gold! We are His oil-burning lamp in the darkness of this world. He actively intercedes for us, His Church, praying for us to grow, mature, live victoriously, and become vessels of His delivering power to the world around us. His residence is permanently inside the heart of the Church. From there, He personally observes and knows our works. And He is always ready to give His truthful, forthright report *with* the delivering power needed to remedy any ill that besets us.

John Transitioned From One Realm to Another Realm

Revelation 2 and 3 reveal some of the challenges the First-Century Church faced. Christ appeared to John on the isle of Patmos, and one of the first things He did was address the issues in each of those seven major churches in Asia — starting with Ephesus.

John said, "I was in the Spirit on the Lord's day..." (Revelation 1:10).

We've learned that this word "was" is the Greek word *ginomai*. It describes *an unexpected or surprising transition from one realm into another realm.* Basically, John said, "I don't know how it happened. It took me completely off guard. I could never replicate this experience if I tried. *Somehow*, I found myself suddenly transitioning from one realm to another realm."

In one moment John was in the cave. The next moment, he had crossed the line that separates the natural realm from the spirit realm. John said, "I was in the spirit." The Greek simply says, "I came to find myself in *a spiritual dimension*."

John Recognized Jesus' Voice

John related that in that realm of the spirit, "...[I] heard behind me a great voice, as of a trumpet, saying, I am Alpha and Omega, the first and the last: and, What thou seest, write in a book, and send it unto the seven churches which are in Asia..." (Revelation 1:10, 11).

John then said, "…I turned to see the voice that spake with me. And being turned, I saw seven golden candlesticks; and in the midst of the seven candlesticks one like unto the Son of man, clothed with a garment down to the foot, and girt about the paps with a golden girdle" (Revelation 1:12, 13).

John intimately knew the voice of Jesus. He had followed Jesus in His earthly ministry and loved Him devotedly. That is why he *turned* to see the One who was speaking to him. John recognized that voice! But as John turned, he expected to see the Jesus he'd known and loved as he walked with Him years before as one of Jesus' 12 disciples — "the disciple whom Jesus loved" (*see* John 13:23; 20:2; 21:20).

When John turned and actually saw the One who was speaking to him in that vision, he was taken aback. John said he saw One who *looked like* the Son of man, but Jesus' appearance had *changed*. Immediately, Jesus began to reveal Himself to John in a way he had never seen — in His Lord's glorified, exalted state.

That is what the word "revelation" means. It is the Greek word *apokalupsis*. The word *apo* means *away*, and *kalupsis* means *something veiled*. When the two words are compounded, it means *to remove the veil* or *pull back the curtains*. This new view of Jesus that John was seeing had been previously hidden. However, in that moment, the Holy Spirit pulled back the curtains, and John saw characteristics of Christ he had never seen before.

John Came Face to Face With Jesus as Our High Priest

The first thing John noticed about Christ was that He was "…clothed with a garment down to the foot, and girt about the paps with a golden girdle" (Revelation 1:13). Interestingly, even though the churches had problems that Jesus was well aware of, He did not distance Himself from them. He was not ashamed of them or mad at them. Instead, He was right in the center of the churches. And notice how He was clothed: *"with a garment down to the foot."* The word "foot" in the original language describes *the naked foot with no shoe*. His garment went down to the bare foot. This clothing describes the attire of the high priest as pictured in Exodus 28.

Jesus revealed Himself to John as *our Great High Priest*. He didn't appear with a sword in His hand or come as Judge to render a verdict and exact punishment. Instead, He appeared as our Great High Priest, and He was standing in prayer for the churches.

What Christ was doing in this passage is what He is still doing today. He loves the Church and is ever interceding for His Church. And since *Jesus* is praying for the Church, *we* need to be praying for the Church too.

From the Outside to the Inside

In Revelation 2:1, Jesus gives us a descriptive picture of Himself as He gave John the following instruction: "Unto the angel of the church of Ephesus write; these things saith he that holdeth the seven stars in his right hand, who *walketh* in the midst of the seven golden candlesticks."

Notice once more the word "walketh." It is the Greek word *peripateo*, which means *to move your feet and walk around*, *to walk circles around*, or *to habitually walk in one area.* It signifies *the vicinity where you live* or *where you are every day.* This is where we find Christ regularly walking — in the midst of His churches today.

As Jesus walked around those seven churches in Asia, He was no doubt getting an outward view of all that was happening. But because an outward view wasn't enough, He came right into the midst of them. This is confirmed by His use of the word "midst," from the Greek word *mesos*, meaning *the very center*, *right into the heart*, *right into the very gut* of the church. That is where Christ habitually walks and strolls. The churches are His place of habitual presence.

To be clear, Christ absolutely loves the Church! That is why He described the seven churches in Revelation 1 and 2 as "golden" candlesticks. "Golden" is the Greek word *chrusos*, which is *gold* — the most valuable commodity of the First Century. By using the word "golden," Jesus was and is saying that the Church is *extremely valuable*, *rare*, and *highly prized.* To Him, there is nothing more precious than His Church.

He Loves Us in Spite of Our Problems

Without question, the Early Church had flaws — and the Church today has flaws too. The Church is filled with imperfect people. From our human viewpoint, that is all we tend to see: problems, weaknesses, inconsistencies, carnality, lack of spirituality, and the list goes on and on. To the natural eye, it can be quite disturbing. Things looked much the same in the

First-Century Church, at the time of John's writing, as they appear to us today.

In Revelation 2 and 3, we see that all seven churches were dealing with *something*. Ephesus had left its first love. Smyrna was suffering intense persecution. The church of Pergamum was tolerating false doctrine — the doctrine of the Nicolaitans. Thyatira was allowing a woman named Jezebel to teach and seduce the congregation. The church of Sardis had a reputation for being spiritually alive, but it was actually in the process of dying. The church of Philadelphia was a good church, but it was very small and had only a little power.

The final church mentioned in that passage was the church of Laodicea. It was a very wealthy church, but it had become lukewarm. Somehow Christ had been put out of the church — probably because they'd ceased to hold Him warmly in their hearts — and He was now standing on the outside. He said, "Behold, I stand at the door, and knock: If any man hear my voice, and open the door, I will come in to him, and will sup with him, and he with me" (Revelation 3:20).

So all seven of these churches were troubled. They had defects. Yet in spite of their problems, Jesus called them "golden" (*see* Revelation 2:1), and He loved them.

Why was the Church golden? Christ had paid for it with His own blood. He gave His life on the Cross and was raised back to life. Then He sent His own Spirit to empower the Church, and He is coming back to gather Her to be with Him for eternity.

In Jesus' view, *the Church was and always will be pure gold!*

A Light in the Darkness

The word "candlesticks" is what Jesus used to describe the seven churches. This is the Greek word *luchnia*, which describes *an oil-burning lamp made out of clay*. These clay lamps were very fragile. If you grabbed one of them too tightly or knocked it off the table, you would break it. It was small enough to hold in one's hand and could easily be transported from room to room by its handle.

Each lamp had a reservoir that held valuable oil. It also had a long wick that soaked in the oil at the lamp's base and protruded out of the mouth at the other end. When the end of the oil-soaked wick in the mouth was ignited, it could burn for hours. A small opening at the top of the lamp allowed people to see when it ran out of oil. It could be refilled again and again.

Oil lamps like these were very common in homes and businesses during the First Century. This is the kind of "candlestick" Jesus used to describe the Church.

Just like the seven churches in the book of Revelation, the Church today is the light of the world. We are a container of the "oil" of the Holy Spirit and are a reservoir for the Spirit's power. If we run out of oil, we can be refilled again and again. When our hearts are ignited with the fire of the Holy Spirit, our mouths begin to burn brightly with truth. Through preaching and teaching the Word, God shines His light through us into the darkness of the world.

Christ Knows Our Works

In Revelation 2:2, Jesus began His address to the Church of Ephesus saying, "I know thy works...." The word "know" is the Greek word *oida*, and it means *to see*, *to behold*, *to perceive*, or *to delightfully view*. It can also describe *a scrutinizing look* or *looking with the intent to examine*. It carries the idea of fully viewing or knowing something from personal observation.

What Christ was about to say to Ephesus — and each of the other churches — was not a result of something He'd heard secondhand. Jesus used the word *oida* ("know") because He had observed with His own eyes the goings-on inside those churches.

Remember, Christ had been walking (*peripateo*) in the midst (*mesos*) of those churches. He had walked around and around them and then came inside the very heart of them to observe their activities. After taking a scrutinizing view, He was ready to give a report.

In the original Greek, Jesus actually said, "I know the works of you — the works that are uniquely yours and that make you different from all the other churches." Likewise, Jesus knows the works of *your* church. Furthermore, He knows the works of *you* personally. He has personally observed and taken a scrutinizing look at your life and is ready to give a report.

What does Christ know? Our "works" — the Greek word *erga*, describing some kind of *action*, *deed*, or *activity*. This often referred to a person's *occupation*, *labor*, or *the things produced by his effort or life*. This word is so all-encompassing that it also pictures *actions*, *beliefs*, and *conduct*.

So when Jesus said, "I know thy works," it was the same as His saying, "I know everything there is to know about you. I've seen your life up close with My own eyes, and now I'm going to tell you about your activities and efforts."

Jesus is the same yesterday, today, and forever (*see* Hebrews 13:8). If He knew from up-close, personal observation the "works" of the people of Ephesus and the other six churches, He knows our works too.

STUDY QUESTIONS

Study to shew thyself approved unto God, a workman that needeth not to be ashamed, rightly dividing the word of truth.
— 2 Timothy 2:15

1. The apostle John intimately knew the voice of Jesus. He had spent time with Him in his younger years and had learned to recognize His voice. You, too, can know the voice of Jesus. He is your *Good Shepherd*, and He longs speaks to you through His Holy Spirit. Carefully read John 10:4, 5, 14, 27; John 14:26; 16:12-15; and Isaiah 30:21. Pray and write down what the Holy Spirit reveals to you.
2. The Church is filled with imperfect people who have flaws, and from our human viewpoint, that is all we tend to see. There is one thing we need from God on a daily basis to help us see people that way He sees us. Read First Peter 4:8 and identify this virtue. How can you see this virtue grow in your life? (For help, *see* 1 John 4:11-17.)

PRACTICAL APPLICATION

But be ye doers of the word, and not hearers only, deceiving your own selves.
— James 1:22

1. When Jesus said, "I know thy works," it was the same as Him saying, "I know *everything* there is to know about you. I've seen your life up close with My own eyes." Does knowing this discourage you or encourage you? Explain your response.
2. Hebrews 13:8 says that Jesus is the same yesterday and today and forever. And since He knew from personal observation the "works" of

the people of Ephesus and the other churches, He knows your works too. Stop and think about it. If Jesus were to appear to you *right now* and give you a report of your activities and efforts, in what ways might He *praise* you? In what areas might He call you to *repent* and come up higher? (If you're not sure of what He might say, why not take a moment and ask Him?)

LESSON 6

TOPIC

A Hard-Working Church

SCRIPTURES

1. **Revelation 1:10, 11** — I was in the Spirit on the Lord's day, and heard behind me a great voice, as of a trumpet, saying, I am Alpha and Omega, the first and the last: and, What thou seest, write in a book, and send it unto the seven churches which are in Asia; unto Ephesus, and unto Smyrna, and unto Pergamos, and unto Thyatira, and unto Sardis, and unto Philadelphia, and unto Laodicea.
2. **Revelation 2:1-3** — Unto the angel of the church of Ephesus write; These things saith he that holdeth the seven stars in his right hand, who walketh in the midst of the seven golden candlesticks; I know thy works, and thy labour, and thy patience, and how thou canst not bear them which are evil: and thou hast tried them which say they are apostles, and are not, and hast found them liars: And hast borne, and hast patience, and for my name's sake hast laboured, and hast not fainted.

GREEK WORDS

1. "bear" — (*bastadzo*): to bear in the hands; to bear responsibility; to take upon oneself; it is the picture of one who seriously carries some type of responsibility
2. "evil" — (*kakos*): evil, vile, foul, or destructive; unacceptable thoughts or actions; actions that are harmful, hurtful, or injurious; an action done with evil intent; actions or attitude that result in damage or ruin in one's life or in the life of another

3. "tried" — ϖ (*peiradzo*): an intense examination to prove the fitness of an object; it was used to describe the fiery process of testing and removing impurities from metal in the ancient world; a test that ensured the metal would be strong and durable — and that any object crafted from the metal would hold up under pressure; it was also used to describe the intense examination to test coins to determine whether they were authentic or counterfeit
4. "who say" — (*legontas*): claiming; asserting; saying
5. "apostles" — ϖ (*apostolos*): to send away; the idea of being commissioned and dispatched with authority and power and sent as a personal representative of a powerful figure or as the official representative of a government; a highly authorized envoy or messenger
6. "liars" — (*pseudes*): false, deceitful, untrue; imposters
7. "false apostles" — ϖ (*pseudapostolos*): a phony, fake, pretend apostle; a bogus apostle; describes someone who intentionally represents himself to be an apostle when he is not

SYNOPSIS

The problems of society in the First Century were many and varied. At the *bouleuterion*, meaning *place of the counselors*, members of the city council met regularly to tackle the troubles of the day. It has been approximately 2,000 years since that time, and we are still meeting in various forums trying to solve societal woes and issues of home and family.

In fact, the problems we deal with today are just as great and are growing more intense. The Bible clearly states that at the very end of the age, the time in which we are now living, the ills of society will become more severe than ever before, and the telltale signs of that inspired prediction are all around us.

You don't have to look far to see that people today are deeply confused. They don't know what is right and what is wrong. There is even great confusion over the issue of gender. Thankfully, God has given us solid, sound advice in His Word on how to effectively carry out end-time ministry.

It is no accident that we are living in this age.

The emphasis of this lesson:

God has positioned us for such a time as this to provide answers for those with questions. What He was saying to the Church in John's time is what He is still speaking now, and we need to hear and heed His words.

'In the Spirit on the Lord's Day'

John was exiled for his faith in Christ — banished to the isle of Patmos by the Emperor Domitian. There in that cave, John received a vision of Jesus like he had never seen before. In Revelation 1:10, John said, "I was in the Spirit on the Lord's day...."

As we learned, that doesn't mean he was in the spirit on the Sabbath day or on a Sunday. No, "the Lord's day" is from the Greek word *kuriakos*, and it means *the Imperial Day of the Emperor*. On this day, the entire Roman Empire worshipped the current emperor. They bowed before that emperor's image, burned incense to him, and worshiped him.

It was on this same day that the *true* Emperor — the King of kings and Lord of lords — chose to "pull back the curtains" and allow John to see Him in a brand-new way.

John said, "I *was* in the Spirit...." As we saw, the word "was" is the Greek word *ginomai*, which describes *a transitioning from one realm to another realm*. John was in the natural realm of the cave when suddenly he found himself "in the Spirit." This signifies that the realm he transitioned into was *the spirit realm*. It was in this dimension of the spirit that John heard Christ begin to speak like the sound of a great trumpet, saying, "...I am Alpha and Omega, the first and the last: and, what thou seest, write in a book, and send it unto the seven churches which are in Asia..." (Revelation 1:11).

The churches Jesus referred to were the seven most influential churches in the Roman province of Asia: Ephesus, Smyrna, Pergamum, Thyatira, Sardis, Philadelphia, and Laodicea.

Ephesus Was a Strategic Location

The first message was directed to the church of Ephesus. It was the first church planted and the biggest, most influential congregation in the region. It was from Ephesus that roads spread outward to all major cities. Whatever happened in Ephesus eventually happened in all of Asia. If a new governor came into Asia, his first stop was always in Ephesus. It was a requirement. Even though his office was in Pergamum, he stopped in Ephesus first.

The Lord is always strategic in what He does; nothing He does is by accident. Jesus knew that by establishing the first church in Ephesus, the Gospel would travel to the entire Asian province.

The same is true for your life. God will strategically direct you in everything you do. If you will listen, He will tell you where to go, what to do, and when to do it. He will instruct you when to speak and when to be silent. He has a strategy for everything, and starting His Church in Ephesus was a part of His strategy to reach the entire Roman province of Asia with the Gospel.

Jesus' Personal, Firsthand Knowledge

In Revelation 2:1 and 2, Jesus said, "Unto the angel of the church of Ephesus write; these things saith he that holdeth the seven stars in his right hand, who walketh in the midst of the seven golden candlesticks; *I know thy works*...."

In our last lesson, we discovered the word "know" is the Greek word *oida*, meaning *to see*, *to behold*, *to perceive*, or *to delightfully view*. It carries the idea of *a scrutinizing look* or *looking with the intent to examine*. It denotes *fully viewing and, therefore, experiencing and knowing from personal observation*.

When Jesus said to the church of Ephesus, "I know thy works," He was essentially saying, "What I've seen, I've seen with My own eyes. I didn't receive a report from an angel or from someone's prayer. I've been walking in the very heart of your church, and I have seen by personal observation your 'works.'"

When Jesus said, "I know thy works," He literally said, "I know the works of you." That is the grammatical structure in Greek. He was saying, "I know the works that are unique to you and that make you different from every other church."

The same is true about your church and even about you personally. Jesus knows the works that are unique to you and that make you different from every other believer.

The word "works" is the Greek word *erga*. It describes *some kind of action*, *deed*, or *activity*. It often referred to *a person's occupation*, *labor*, or *the things produced by his efforts in life*. It could describe *the results of hard work or hard labor*. This word is so all-encompassing that it includes *a person's actions, beliefs, and conduct*. By saying, "I know thy works," Jesus said, "I know everything about all your activities and deeds. I've seen it all up close and in person. In fact, there is nothing about you I don't know."

Interestingly, Jesus used this phrase "I know thy works" when He spoke to all seven of the churches of Asia, including Ephesus, Smyrna, Pergamum, Thyatira, Sardis, Philadelphia, and Laodicea. He knows the deeds, activities, and conduct that are unique to every single church and every single believer.

Ephesus Was a Hard-Working Congregation

Jesus said, "I know thy works, and thy *labour*..." (Revelation 2:2). Again, the grammatical structure in Greek indicates that Jesus actually said, "I know the labor that is unique and especially characteristic of you." The word "labour" is the Greek word *kopos*, and it describes *the hardest, most wearisome kind of labor*. It can describe *toil* or *fatigue*. It is *the picture of a person who gives everything to a project or assignment, striving and working with every fiber of his being*. This word often typifies *work that is wearisome, exhausting, and of the hardest kind*. It can be applied to physical, mental, or spiritual effort. This is the word we would all want Jesus to use to describe us.

One thing Christ knew without question was that the Church of Ephesus was hard-working. There was no limitation of desire or effort to work hard and give everything they had to a project. Again, this was the biggest, most influential church in Asia. It was a missionary base where ministry leaders were raised up, trained, and sent out to serve.

Jesus said, "I know the work that is unique to you and that makes you, Ephesus, different from all the other churches. You are a hard-working church, consumed with working for the Kingdom."

Ephesus Was Patient

Just after citing their hard-working nature, Jesus said, "I know your patience. You have a kind of patience that is unique to you." That word "patience" is the Greek word *hupomone*, which means *to stay or remain in one's spot*; *to keep a position*; or *to resolve to maintain territory gained*. The church of Ephesus knew they played a pivotal, unique role in God's plan for Asia, and they refused to abandon it.

In a military sense, *hupomone* ("patience") pictures *soldiers ordered to maintain their positions even in the face of opposition.* It indicates *one who defiantly sticks it out, regardless of pressures mounted against him.* It is *staying power* or *"hang-in-there" power.* It is the attitude that *holds out*, *holds on*, *outlasts*, *perseveres*, and *hangs in there*, *never giving up*, *refusing to surrender to obstacles*, and *turning down every opportunity to quit.* It pictures someone under a heavy load, but who refuses to *bend*, *break*, or *surrende*r because he is convinced that the *territory*, *promise*, or *principle* under assault rightfully belongs to him.

Hupomone is a picture of *great stamina* and *durability.*

Ephesus refused to bend, break or give up. Regardless of the persecution Domitian brought against them, they would not surrender to the pressure. They rejected every opportunity to quit. In all of this, Jesus commended them.

Ephesus Was Responsible and Stood Against Evil

Jesus didn't stop there. In addition to telling the church of Ephesus they were hard-working and patient, He added, "...And how thou canst not bear them which are evil..." (Revelation 2:2). The word "bear" is the Greek word *bastadzo*, which means *to bear responsibility.* It is the picture of *one who seriously carries some type of responsibility.* Ephesus was a very responsible church. They understood God had entrusted them with a special responsibility because they were a big, powerful congregation whose efforts were affecting the entire region.

What could the Ephesians not bear? Those who were "evil" — the Greek word *kakos*, meaning *evil*, *vile*, *foul*, or *destructive.* This evil describes *unacceptable thoughts or actions*; *actions that are harmful*, *hurtful*, or *injurious.* It is *an action done with evil intent*; *an action or attitude that results in damage or ruin in one's life or in the life of another.*

Apparently, a group of people were trying to do something in Ephesus that was evil, foul and destructive (*kakos*). Had the Ephesian believers allowed them to do it, their actions would have had a ruinous influence in many people's lives. For this, Jesus praised them saying, "Wow! You are so responsible. You refused to bear with those who came with an evil intent." The church of Ephesus understood they were the gate-keepers to Asia. Therefore, they were very careful about who they endorsed and sent out to other churches.

They Tested the Authenticity of Apostles

What else did Jesus say to the Church of Ephesus? He commended them again, saying, "…Thou hast *tried* them which say they are apostles, and are not, and hast found them liars…" (Revelation 2:2). The word "tried" is the Greek word *peiradzo*, and it describes *an intense examination to prove the fitness of an object*. It was used to describe *the fiery process of testing and removing impurities from metal in the ancient world*. The word *peiradzo* was also used to describe *the intense examination used to test coins to determine whether they were authentic or counterfeit*.

In other words, when people showed up in Ephesus and said they were apostles, which happened quite frequently, the Ephesian believers didn't just embrace them and say, "Hallelujah! Another apostle has come." Instead, they *tried* them. They put them through intense tests to find out if they were authentic or counterfeit.

In those days, there were a number of bogus apostles — people claiming to be apostles because they wanted the authority and power that came with the position. Apostles often oversaw a large territory, thereby controlling many people. The church of Ephesus was well aware of this and, therefore, "tried" all those who showed up claiming to be apostles with a new revelation.

Again, the church of Ephesus was very responsible (*bastadzo*). They took their position in the Kingdom very seriously. They understood that if they put their stamp of approval on someone, they would be endorsing a person who would ultimately take his message throughout Asia. For this reason, they tried "them which say they are apostles." The Greek meaning for "which say" is *those who claim or assert to be apostles*, yet they often were not.

These imposters in Revelation 2:2 were "found" to be "liars." The word "found" is the Greek word *heurisko*, and it means *to find or to discover*; *a discovery made as a result of careful observance*. It is *the moment when one makes a surprising or conclusive discovery*.

Heurisko is actually the word from which we get the saying, "*Eureka!*" which means, "I found it!"

After putting "them which say they are apostles" through an intense examination, questioning them and listening to their responses — *eureka!* — they discovered the truth: Those so-called apostles were nothing but "liars" —

the Greek word *pseudes*, meaning *false*, *deceitful*, or *untrue*; *imposters*. And through the thorough investigation by the Ephesian church, the frauds were stopped dead in their tracks from further propagating their lies.

Jesus praised the church of Ephesus for their extreme work ethic, their patient endurance and stamina, and their unwillingness to tolerate or endorse those bent on evil. Instead, they put people to the test to find out if they were authentic or counterfeit. Indeed, Ephesus was a magnificent church.

Yet Jesus did have something against them. We'll cover that in the next lesson.

STUDY QUESTIONS

Study to shew thyself approved unto God, a workman that needeth not to be ashamed, rightly dividing the word of truth.
— 2 Timothy 2:15

1. The Lord is always strategic in what He does. Nothing is by accident or coincidence. He is guiding you. If you will listen, He will tell you *where to go*, *what to do*, and *when to do it*. He will instruct you when to be silent, when to speak, and even give you the words to say (*see* Proverbs 16:9 and 20:24; Psalm 25:9, 12 and 32:8; Matthew 10:19, 20; and Luke 12:11, 12). Meditate on these promises and write down what the Lord speaks to you through them.
2. God's Word declares "The heart is deceitful above all things, and desperately wicked: who can know it?" (Jeremiah 17:9) Thankfully, in the very next verse, He encourages us with the news that He is able to search our hearts and reveal them to us. Take a moment and mediate on David's prayer in Psalm 139:23 and 24 and make it your own. Ask the Lord to search your heart right now and show you anything you need to be aware and deal with at this time. (Also consider Psalm 26:2; Hebrews 4:12, 13.)

PRACTICAL APPLICATION

But be ye doers of the word, and not hearers only, deceiving your own selves.
— James 1:22

1. In describing the church of Ephesus, Jesus applauded them for being *hard-working*, *patient*, and *responsible*. He praised them for *testing the character* of those who claimed to be mature Christian leaders and exposing those who were counterfeits. Which of these characteristics might Jesus use to define *you*? In what other ways might He describe the uniqueness of *your* works?
2. The church of Ephesus clearly knew the responsibility with which they had been entrusted. Do you know the responsibility the Lord has entrusted to *your church*? That is, what seems to be the specific area of gifting in which your church has been called to function? How about to you personally? What specific area of gifting has the Lord entrusted to you? Briefly describe what you know about each.

LESSON 7

TOPIC

How Does Anyone Leave a First Love?

SCRIPTURES

1. **Revelation 2:1-5** — Unto the angel of the church of Ephesus write; These things saith he that holdeth the seven stars in his right hand, who walketh in the midst of the seven golden candlesticks; I know thy works, and thy labour, and thy patience, and how thou canst not bear them which are evil: and thou hast tried them which say they are apostles, and are not, and hast found them liars: And hast borne, and hast patience, and for my name's sake hast laboured, and hast not fainted. Nevertheless I have somewhat against thee, because thou hast left thy first love. Remember therefore from whence thou art fallen, and repent, and do the first works; or else I will come unto thee quickly, and will remove thy candlestick out of his place, except thou repent.
2. **Revelation 1:10, 11** — I was in the Spirit on the Lord's day, and heard behind me a great voice, as of a trumpet, saying, I am Alpha and Omega, the first and the last: and, What thou seest, write in a book, and send it unto the seven churches which are in Asia; unto Ephesus,

and unto Smyrna, and unto Pergamos, and unto Thyatira, and unto Sardis, and unto Philadelphia, and unto Laodicea.

GREEK WORDS

1. "hast borne" — (*bastadzo*): to bear in the hands; to bear responsibility; to take upon oneself; pictures one who seriously carries some type of responsibility
2. "hast patience" — ϖ μ (*hupomone*): to stay or abide; to remain in one's spot; to keep a position; to resolve to maintain territory gained; in a military sense, it pictures soldiers ordered to maintain their positions even in the face of opposition; to defiantly stick it out regardless of pressures mounted against it; staying power; "hang-in-there" power; the attitude that holds out, holds on, outlasts, perseveres, and hangs in there, never giving up, refusing to surrender to obstacles, and turning down every opportunity to quit; pictures one under a heavy load, but who refuses to bend, break, or surrender because he is convinced that the territory, promise, or principle under assault rightfully belongs to him; stamina; durability
3. "hast laboured" — ϖ (*kopos*): the hardest and most wearisome kind of labor; toil; fatigue; the picture of one who gives everything to a project or assignment — one who strives and works with every fiber of his being; typifies work that may be wearisome or exhausting; the hardest kind of labor; can be applied to physical, mental, or spiritual effort
4. "fainted" — ϖ (*kopiao*): pictures weariness to the point of exhaustion; to grow physically, mentally, and emotionally tired as a result of continual, unending work
5. "I have" — (*echo*): to embrace something tightly; to firmly grip an object or ideal so tightly that no one can take it away from you; to keep, protect, possess
6. "against" — (*kata*): a downward strike; a strike against
7. "left" — μ (*aphiemi*): not the deliberate abandonment of a thing, but the involuntary, unintentional release of something once held dear; to neglect; to ignore; to unintentionally leave something or someone behind
8. "first" — ϖ (*protos*): first; early; preeminent

9. "love"— ϖ (*agape*): a divine love that gives and gives, even if it's never responded to, thanked, or acknowledged; this love occurs when an individual sees, recognizes, understands, or appreciates the value of an object or a person, causing the viewer to behold this object or person in great esteem, awe, admiration, wonder, and sincere appreciation; such great respect is awakened in the heart of the observer for the object or person he is beholding that he is compelled to love it; a love for a person or object that is irresistible; a love so profound that it knows no limits or boundaries in how far — wide, high, and deep — it will go to show that love to its recipient; a self-sacrificial love that moves the lover to action

SYNOPSIS

During early New Testament times, the city of Ephesus had a population of about 250,000. In the middle of this thriving city was a powerful church — the church of Ephesus. It was a mission church involved in planting churches all over Asia, including churches in Smyrna, Pergamum, Thyatira, Sardis, Philadelphia, and Laodicea. This was an active, on-fire church.

Jesus had many great things to say about the church of Ephesus. Yet He had one thing against them that was personally heartbreaking: The believers in Ephesus had lost their first love. After faithfully serving Christ and pouring out their lives to see His Kingdom advanced, their love and excitement for Him was waning. Jesus was calling them to repent and return to Him, their first love.

The emphasis of this lesson:

The church of Ephesus was doing incredible things for Christ. They were deeply committed, exercising great patience, maintaining doctrinal integrity, and working extremely hard to advance His Kingdom. But they had lost their first love. Sometimes we, too, lose our passion for Christ, just as the believers of Ephesus did. In those moments, He calls us to repent and return to Him. Through repentance, we can regain our excitement and love for Jesus and continue to effectively fulfill His calling on our lives.

John Was in the Spirit

In Revelation 1:10, the apostle John said, "I was in the Spirit on the Lord's day, and heard behind me a great voice, as of a trumpet, saying, I am Alpha and Omega, the first and the last: and, What thou seest, write in a book, and send it unto the seven churches which are in Asia; unto Ephesus, and unto Smyrna, and unto Pergamos, and unto Thyatira, and unto Sardis, and unto Philadelphia, and unto Laodicea."

John said, "I was in the Spirit." The word "was" is the Greek word *ginomai*, which describes *a transition from one realm into another realm*. This word signifies *an element of surprise*. It was as if John was saying, "I don't know how it happened, and I could never replicate it. But suddenly and unexpectedly, I found myself in another dimension."

The phrase "in the Spirit" indicates the dimension into which he transitioned. It was *the realm of the spirit*. Another translation of this phrase could read, "I came to find myself in the spirit realm — in a spiritual dimension." It was in the realm of the spirit that John heard Jesus' familiar voice spoken in a different way, and received a brand-new revelation of His exalted Lord.

Ephesus: the Doorway to Asia

As we've seen throughout these lessons, the city of Ephesus was strategic to the entire Roman province in Asia politically, educationally, and spiritually. The mindset was, if you were successful in Ephesus, the door was open for you to go anywhere you desired in the region. Whatever gained acceptance in Ephesus eventually permeated all of Asia.

Spiritually, this was good. The Holy Spirit strategically directed the apostle Paul to begin ministering in Ephesus. God knew that once the Gospel was established there, the doorway to all of Asia would be open to it, and that is exactly what took place. The church of Ephesus became the biggest, most notable and influential of all the churches in Asia. From there, churches were birthed in Smyrna, Pergamum, Thyatira, Sardis, Philadelphia, and Laodicea.

The downside to Ephesus being the doorway was that it also became a place for spiritual opportunists to come and peddle their new revelations. If a person could "score big" in the church of Ephesus, it would throw open the door for them to minister freely in *all* the churches in the province. This motivated many so-called apostles to come to Ephesus from all over the Roman Empire to try out their strange revelations.

The believers in Ephesus grew wise to what was happening. They swiftly rose to the occasion and put safeguards in place to effectively put a stop to pretend apostles trying to infiltrate the church. This was one of the attributes for which Jesus praised the church of Ephesus.

Christ's Commendation of Ephesus

As John was in the realm of the spirit, Jesus spoke words of commendation and correction regarding the seven major churches in Asia, and He began by addressing the "angel" at the Ephesian church, which we learned was the *pastor* of that work.

Jesus said, "I know thy works…" (Revelation 2:2). The word "know" is the Greek word *oida*, which means *to see, behold, perceive*, or *delightfully view*. It describes *a scrutinizing look or a look with the intent to examine and fully view*. The word *oida* also means *to experience or know something from personal observation*.

What did Jesus "know" (*oida*)? He knew the "works" of the church of Ephesus. "Works" is the Greek word *erga*, and it describes *the total output of a person's life — his actions, deeds, or activities*. It often referred to *a person's occupation, profession, and labor* and denoted *the result of hard work*. The word *erga* was so all-encompassing that it pictured *the totality of a person's actions, beliefs, and conduct*.

When Christ said, "I know thy works," it was like He said, "I know every single thing about you — all your actions, deeds, beliefs, and conduct. There's nothing about you I don't know. And it all came from My personal observation of you. Now I'm going to give you a report of My findings."

Let's take a closer look from Scripture at what Christ "knew" about the church of Ephesus.

1. **"I know…thy labour."** This was the first commendation Jesus noted. The Greek word for "labour" is *kopos*, and it describes *the hardest, most wearisome kind of labor*. It can be applied to physical, mental, or spiritual effort. It also indicates *toil* or *fatigue* or *one who gives everything he has to a project or assignment*. The word *kopos* can describe *a person who has become weary or exhausted because he has worked so hard, with every fiber of his being*.

Using the word *kopos* was a huge compliment to the Ephesian believers. It is what we would want Jesus to say about us. This church was extremely hard-working and deeply committed. They gave everything they had to accomplish whatever task was in front of them.

2. **"I know…thy patience."** This was the second quality Jesus praised. "Patience" is the Greek word *hupomone*, which means *to stay, abide, or remain in one's spot*. It is an attitude that says, "I'm not budging. This is my spot, and I'm not moving." This word signifies *a resolve to maintain territory gained*, which is what the church of Ephesus had done.

   In a military sense, *hupomone* — the word "patience" — *depicted soldiers who were ordered to maintain their positions, even in the face of fierce combat*. They were to stick it out regardless of the pressure mounted against them. *Hupomone* is *staying power* or *"hang-in-there" power*. It is *the attitude that holds on, holds out, outlasts, perseveres, and never gives up*. When given the opportunity to surrender, that opportunity is flatly rejected. *Hupomone* then becomes *the picture of one who is under a heavy load, but refuses to bend, break, or surrender because he is convinced that the territory, promise, or principle under assault rightly belongs to him.*

   The church of Ephesus served as the gatekeeper of Asia, and they were under assault. In addition to being persecuted, they were also being inundated with people claiming to be apostles. The temptation was to give up under the weariness and exhaustion of their labor. However, they had made a decision to operate in "patience" (*hupomone*). They would not bend, break, or surrender. Like good soldiers, they dug in their heels and effectively maintained their positions. This is what Christ has called us to do as well.

3. **"I know…how thou canst not bear them which are evil."** The word "bear" is the Greek word *bastadzo*, which means *to bear responsibility for something*. The word "evil" is the Greek word *kakos*, and it describes something *evil*, *vile*, *foul*, or *destructive*; *something that is unacceptable in thought or action*. It also indicates *actions that are harmful, hurtful, or injurious or done with evil intent*. Actions or attitudes like these result in damage and can even ruin one's life or the life of another.

   Evidently, someone was trying to do something in the church of Ephesus that was evil, and Jesus commended the Ephesian leaders saying, "You refused to endorse it. You would not tolerate those who were bent on doing evil, and you've done well."

4. **"I know...thou hast tried them which say they are apostles, and are not, and hast found them liars."** Jesus also praised the church of Ephesus for identifying the false apostles. He said, "Thou hast tried them." The word "tried" is the Greek word *peiradzo,* and it describes *an intense examination often used to test coins to determine whether they were authentic or counterfeit.* When someone came and claimed to be an apostle with a new revelation, the Ephesian leaders would question them, probing them doctrinally and spiritually to determine if they were authentic or counterfeit.

   Who were they testing? Jesus said, "...them which say they are apostles...." "Which say" means *claiming, asserting,* or *pretending* to be apostles. Why were so many desiring to be recognized as apostles? Apostles were given great authority over many people in a large territory. Power-hungry people who wanted to control and manipulate others saw this as a golden opportunity and attempted to seize it.

   However, about those false apostles, the Ephesian believers "found them liars." The word "found" is the Greek word *heurisko*, which means *to find or discover through careful observation after an intense investigation, scientific study, or scholarly research.* This word "liars" is the Greek word *pseudes*, which means *imposters.* These so-called apostles were nothing more than *bogus pretenders* who were striving for self-promotion and selfish gain.

For all these wonderful attributes, Jesus commended the church of Ephesus.

Christ Had Something Against the Church of Ephesus

The focus changes in Revelation 2:4. Here Jesus said, "Nevertheless I have somewhat against thee, *because thou hast left thy first love.*" In spite of all the good things Jesus had said about this outstanding church congregation, there was something Jesus needed to address. *The church of Ephesus had left their first love.*

How did that happen? How could a church so on fire, so committed, so resolved to maintaining their position and not allowing phony apostles to spread lies leave their first love? In the original Greek, this phrase "because thou hast left thy first love" actually says, "Because your love, the first one, you have left." The phrase "the first one" could also be translated "the early one."

Jesus was referring to what the Ephesian believers were like when they first repented and came to Him. He was reminding them of the deep admiration, esteem, appreciation, wonder, and awe that was awakened in their hearts when they first received Him as Savior and Lord years earlier.

Like young people who fall in love, the Ephesians initially fell *head over heels* in love with Jesus. Their hearts were captivated with love for Him, and there were no limits to what they would do to express their love for Him. They were willing to sacrifice everything to follow Him. But by the time John received his revelation on the isle of Patmos, more than 30 years had passed, and the Ephesians' love was not the same.

Jesus said, "Nevertheless I have somewhat against you…." The phrase, "I have" is the Greek word *echo*, which means *to hold something tightly in a very personal way*. What Christ was about to describe was something He felt very personally. The word "against" is the Greek term *kata*, and it describes *a downward strike*. By using this word, it is as if Jesus was saying, "With all the good things I've already said about you, there is one strike I personally hold against you."

What did He hold against them? Notice the phrase "you have left." The word "left" is the Greek word *aphiemi*, which signifies *the involuntary release of something once held dear*. It means *to neglect, to ignore, or to unintentionally leave something*. The church of Ephesus had become so involved in the machinery of the ministry — like many of us do — that they lost the wonder and awe of when they first came to Christ. They were still committed, still exercising patience, still maintaining doctrinal integrity, and still working extremely hard, but they were no longer captivated with deep admiration and appreciation for Jesus.

What was the remedy? "Remember therefore from whence thou art fallen, and repent, and do the first works…" (Revelation 2:5). What Christ said to Ephesus, He is, in effect, saying to us today: "In all your serving, don't surrender the wonder of knowing and loving Me."

If you have lost your first preoccupation of loving Jesus, He says, "Repent and return to Me."

STUDY QUESTIONS

Study to shew thyself approved unto God, a workman that needeth not to be ashamed, rightly dividing the word of truth.
— 2 Timothy 2:15

1. When God initially calls us to a task, we are usually excited and invigorated by the opportunity. Over time, however, our passion can become diminished by the challenges that arise — especially by the enemy's assault against us. Are you weary in well-doing? Do you need *fresh energy* for the work God has called you to do? Take a few moments to read these amazing promises in Isaiah 40:28-31, Ephesians 3:16, Philippians 4:13, and Second Corinthians 12:9 and 10. Write out the one that speaks to you most.
2. The Ephesians worked hard at preserving doctrinal integrity. Through intense investigation and examination, they tested those who claimed to be apostles and discovered through their investigation whether they were counterfeit or authentic. According to First John 4:1-6, how can you know if a person is of God or *not* of God — or whether someone is a genuine believer, but is nevertheless misguided in his or her ambitions? Describe the characteristics of both honoring God's plan through authenticity and *dis*honoring it through selfish ambition. (Also consider 1 Thessalonians 5:21.)

PRACTICAL APPLICATION

But be ye doers of the word, and not hearers only, deceiving your own selves.
—James 1:22

1. The church of Ephesus exercised "patience" (*hupomone*). Although they were under a heavy load, they refused to bend, break, or surrender. They were convinced that the territory and promises God had given them rightly belonged to them, and they refused to budge from where God had called them. How about you? In what ways do you need to exercise patience?
2. When it came to guarding doctrinal integrity, remaining deeply committed, exercising patience, and working hard, few churches could compare with the church of Ephesus. Yet somewhere along the way, they became so involved in the machinery of ministry that they lost

the wonder and awe of when they first came to Christ. Be honest: Have you lost your first love for Jesus? Take a few moments to reflect on the attitude and demeanor you had when you first came to Him. Describe what you were like *then* in comparison to what you are like *now.*

3. Based on your answer to the previous question, is there anything you sense the Holy Spirit prompting you to do? If so, write what it is and ask Him for the grace to carry it out.

LESSON 8

TOPIC

Remember

SCRIPTURES

1. **Hebrews 10:32** — But call to remembrance the former days, in which, after ye were illuminated, ye endured a great fight of afflictions.
2. **Revelation 2:1-5** — Unto the angel of the church of Ephesus write; These things saith he that holdeth the seven stars in his right hand, who walketh in the midst of the seven golden candlesticks; I know thy works, and thy labour, and thy patience, and how thou canst not bear them which are evil: and thou hast tried them which say they are apostles, and are not, and hast found them liars: And hast borne, and hast patience, and for my name's sake hast laboured, and hast not fainted. Nevertheless I have somewhat against thee, because thou hast left thy first love. Remember therefore from whence thou art fallen, and repent, and do the first works; or else I will come unto thee quickly, and will remove thy candlestick out of his place, except thou repent.

GREEK WORDS

1. "remember" — **μ** (*mneia*): denotes a written record used to memorialize a person's actions; often signified a statue, monument, or some type of memorial that was intended to be permanent; to recollect, mention, commemorate, or memorialize
2. "whence" — ϖ (*pothen*): points back to a different place or time

3. "fallen" — ϖ ϖ (*pipto*): to fall; to collapse; to fall into a terrible predicament or into a worse state than one was in before; depicts someone who falls into some type of failure; a downward plummet; often used to depict a person who falls so hard that it appears he has fallen dead like a corpse; pictures a downfall from a presumed high and haughty position

SYNOPSIS

In the Roman province of Asia, there is road called the Royal Road. It began at the harbor in the city of Smyrna and extended all the way to the land of Persia. Kings, queens, emperors, dignitaries, and politicians all traveled this road. What makes it so unique is that there are ancient tombs situated along this road — tombs that date back as far as four centuries before Christ.

As people traveled this road, they would often take time to stop and look at the tombs. In these graves are the remains of illustrious historians, military officers, soldiers, and other legendary figures. The purpose of placing their tombs along the Royal Road was to remind travelers of the great people who also once passed that way.

The Greek word used to describe these tombs is *mneia*. It signifies *a tomb*, *sepulcher*, *monument*, or *grave*, and it is a word used throughout the New Testament. One such place is Hebrews 10:32, which says, "But call to remembrance the former days…." By using the word "remembrance" (*mneia*), the Holy Spirit is telling us there are some things that once passed our way that we should never forget. If we have buried good memories of what God has done in our lives, we need to unearth them and put them in a place where we can easily observe and appreciate them regularly.

The emphasis of this lesson:

The Ephesian believers had forgotten many of the great experiences they had with God when they first came to Christ. Amidst all the busyness of their lives, these memories had become buried. Jesus told them, "Remember therefore from whence thou art fallen…" (Revelation 2:5). We, too, are to call to remember the great things God has done for us — we are to mentally position them around us so we can easily revisit them often.

Jesus Brought Commendation to the Church of Ephesus

In Revelation 2:1, Jesus was speaking to the "angel" of the church of Ephesus — the Greek word *angelos* — which, in this passage means *the messenger of the church* or *the pastor*. This demonstrates that Jesus honors and never bypasses the authority He has established in the church. The pastor is the head of a local church, so if something needs to be said to that congregation, Jesus will speak first to him. The pastor is then responsible to processes it and share it with the people.

What did Jesus say to the pastor of the church of Ephesus? "I know thy works, and thy labour, and thy patience, and how thou canst not bear them which are evil: and thou hast tried them which say they are apostles, and are not, and hast found them liars" (Revelation 2:2).

In our last lesson, we learned that because Ephesus was the doorway to the province of Asia, it was a strategic location educationally, politically, and spiritually. People knew that if they could make a name for themselves in Ephesus, the rest of the province would be open to them. As a result, many would-be apostles from all over the Roman Empire began traveling to Ephesus with the motive in mind to garner the approval and endorsement of the church leaders.

The Ephesian elders soon became aware of what was happening and put safeguards in place to filter out the phonies and to preserve doctrinal integrity and protect the rest of the congregation. They were never quick to lay hands on newcomers and give them their endorsement. Instead, they "tried them which say they are apostles." Through intense examination and questioning, leaders were able to determine who was authentic and who was counterfeit. In the process, many were found to be liars.

The word "liars" is the Greek word *pseudes*, which means *imposters*. These so-called apostles were nothing more than *bogus pretenders*. Of course, not everyone who came to Ephesus had selfish, evil motives for wanting to become an apostle, but many were revealed to be counterfeits after being investigated by the church leaders.

Jesus praised the church of Ephesus for its diligence in this area as well as other areas. In Revelation 2:3, He added, "And hast borne, and hast patience, and for my name's sake hast laboured, and hast not fainted." The phrase "hast borne" is a form of the same Greek word for "bear" — it is the word *bastadzo*. In this verse, the Greek actually says, "You have *continually* borne the responsibility you were given; you did not abdicate or relinquish it." Likewise, the phrase "hast patience" is from the Greek word for "patience," *hupomone*. In this verse, that word could also be translated, "You have *continually* stayed under a heavy load, refusing to bend and refusing to break. Even though you felt like throwing in the towel at times, you didn't. You refused to quit."

What else did Jesus credit the Ephesus believers with doing for His name's sake? He said they "hast laboured, and hast not fainted." The phrase, "hast laboured" is taken from the Greek word *kopos*. In this verse, it could be accurately translated as, "You have *continued* to labor with the hardest, most wearisome kind of labor."

Not only that, but Jesus commended this congregation for not fainting. The phrase, "and hast not fainted" means *they didn't give up or give out.* Even weary with exhaustion, having grown tired at times physically and mentally and emotionally, these believers vigorously stayed put at their posts.

Indeed, the church of Ephesus had cultivated many attributes for which Jesus commended them. However, there was one thing He held against them. And in bringing His accurate report based on His own observations, He also brought *correction*, along with *commendation*, to this body of believers.

Jesus Also Brought *Correction* to the Ephesus Church

In Revelation 2:4 Jesus said, "Nevertheless I have somewhat against thee, because thou hast left thy first love." This word "nevertheless" presents a break in the text. It is the Greek word *alla*, and it could be translated as, "*In spite of all these wonderful things,* I have something else to say."

First, Jesus said, "I have somewhat against thee...." The phrase "I have" is the Greek word *echo*, meaning *to firmly have* or *to hold something very personally*. Jesus was literally saying, "There is something that I have against you, and I'm holding it very personally. It's something I feel deeply." This thing He held was something that was very disturbing to the Lord.

Next is the word "against," which is the Greek word *kata*. It describes *a downward mark or a strike against somebody.* In other words, Jesus was saying, "With all the great things I've said about you, there is one thing I'm holding that is a strike against you, and I feel it very deeply."

What was the strike against the Church of Ephesus Jesus felt so deeply? He said, "...Because thou hast left thy first love."

Interestingly, the structure in the Greek is different than the sentence reads. The phrase, "Because thou hast left thy first love" actually says, "Because your love — the first one — you have left." The words "the first one" is a Greek phrase meaning *early love.* It is the kind of love experienced between two young people who have just fallen deeply in love. They long to be around each other all the time. When they're apart, they count the moments until they can be together again. Jesus said, "Your *early love* — the awe and wonder you carried in your heart when you first came to Me — you've left it."

Notice that the word "left" doesn't mean *abandoned.* Instead, it is the Greek word *aphiemi*, and it denotes *the involuntary release of something you once held very dear and close to your heart.* You see, over a period of time, the church of Ephesus had become so involved in the machinery of ministry and the busyness of life that they began to lose their personal vibrancy for Jesus. Although they were deeply involved in church activity, they had drifted from the Lord Himself. Somehow they allowed the wonder of who He was to slip through their grasp and become loosened from their hearts.

How Does One Leave His First Love?

By the time the apostle John saw Jesus on the isle of Patmos, more than 30 years had passed since the Ephesians had first repented and come to Christ as brand-new believers. Although they were still deeply committed to the Lord, they no longer held the deep, fiery passion for Him that previously burned in their hearts. How did that happen? What events took place that led to their love growing cold?

Rick explains it best in his book *A Light in Darkness: Seven Messages to the Seven Churches*:

> Over the years, as they [the Ephesians] became more doctrinally sophisticated and astute, their simple but profound first love for Jesus had somehow dissipated and slipped away from them, even though they never stopped faithfully serving Him....

This was still a remarkable church, but the spiritual fervency that characterized this body of believers in the past was now missing…. It often happens that the first generation of Christians during a move of God experiences dramatic salvations as that segment of the Church is born in the power of the Spirit. However, the second generation, raised in a Christian environment, often doesn't experience the same radical deliverance their parents did….

As each successive generation becomes more accustomed to a Christian environment — learning to speak the language of the church, sing the songs of the church, and act the way "church" people should act — it becomes easy for the younger generations to slip into a mindset of familiarity.

Too often this can produce apathy in people's hearts, ultimately leading them to take the redemptive work of Christ for granted. Therefore, the potential for spiritual fires to grow dimmer increases dangerously with each new successive generation — *unless* each church and its members become unrelenting in their commitment to retain their spiritual passion for Christ….

Therefore He urged them [the church of Ephesus] to "remember."

When a church becomes older and more structured, polished, refined, and doctrinally developed, it can become so engaged in ministry business that it runs the risk of forfeiting its zeal and spiritual fire. What was once held as precious often becomes routine. And as the leadership and church members become accustomed to the precious Holy Spirit in their lives, too often they unintentionally begin to simply 'traffic' in the things of God….

In its early years, this church [the Ephesian church] burned like a spiritual inferno, and the vibrancy and excitement of these Ephesian believers inspired the same passion in other churches and spiritual leaders. But as the years passed, the zeal the church once possessed for the things of God slowly ebbed away. Knowledge increased, but the believers' fiery passion for Jesus diminished….

The Ephesians were so busy serving Jesus that they lost their intimacy with Him…. For this reason, Jesus went on to say, "*Remember* therefore from whence thou art fallen..." (v. 5). Christ

> urged them to stop everything they were doing to 'remember' the precious fellowship they used to enjoy with Him....[1]

The truth is, we all run the risk of becoming so busy serving Jesus that we lose our intimacy with Him. What once was precious can easily become predictable and routine.

What is the remedy for such a dreadful spiritual tragedy? *Remembering.*

'Remember Therefore From Whence Thou Art Fallen'

Jesus told the church of Ephesus, "Remember therefore from whence thou art fallen, and repent, and do the first works..." (Revelation 2:5). This word "remember" comes from the Greek word *mneia*. This word denotes *a written record to memorialize a person's actions*. It often signifies *a sepulcher*, *a statue*, *a monument*, or *a tombstone* — similar to those graves that could be seen on the Royal Road.

The word "whence" is the Greek word *pothen*, which means *to point back to a different place or a different time*. Basically, Jesus was saying, "Put everything else on pause and mentally go back to the beginning of your relationship with Me. Remember the vibrancy of your love and the excitement you once had. And if you have *fallen* from that experience, *repent*."

The word "fallen" is the Greek word *pipto*. It describes *a fall*, *a collapse*, or *a downward plummet*. This word was often used to depict *a person who falls so hard that it appears he has fallen dead like a corpse*. It also indicates *someone who falls from a formerly high and haughty position*. The church of Ephesus had a glorious past and a rich reputation. In the eyes of the church world, they were the greatest. They had become the model church of sophistication and development. But Jesus saw the real picture. They had fallen from the zeal and spiritual passion they once possessed, and it hurt Him personally.

The early experiences the Ephesian believers shared with Christ had become buried by more than 30 years of spiritual activity. Jesus was urging them to "remember" (*mneia*) what they once shared together — to dig through the clutter of their schedules, activities, and routines in order to unearth their precious memories of intimacy together with Him. Once they dug deep and *remembered* the times when their faith was tender and new, they would be able to see how far they had drifted from the fervent love they once had for Christ — and then return to Him.

What God had done in the lives of the Ephesian believers was wonderful, and those memories needed to be memorialized — *remembered* — among them for all generations. Yes, testing the authenticity of apostles, remaining steadfast at their spiritual posts, refusing to give up territory they had gained, raising up spiritual leaders, starting new churches, and working tirelessly to advance the Kingdom of God were all spiritual feats and traits to be admired. And Jesus indeed *commended* them for all these things. But none of their spiritual activity was a substitute for the loving, intimate connection they once shared with Him.

What Jesus said to the Ephesian believers, He says to you today: "It's time to put everything else on pause and remember when you first came to Me and fell in love with Me. Remember the joy of our fellowship that energized your every thought. Go back to the beginning and recall what we shared together — the power of My Spirit infusing and energizing your life and how you were changed. Don't lose the wonder of it all. *Remember!*"

STUDY QUESTIONS

Study to shew thyself approved unto God, a workman that needeth not to be ashamed, rightly dividing the word of truth.
— 2 Timothy 2:15

1. The psalmist said, "I will remember the works of the Lord: surely I will remember thy wonders of old. I will meditate also of all thy work, and talk of thy doings" (Psalm 77:11, 12). Think for a moment. What are some positive benefits of *remembering*, *meditating on*, and *telling others about* God's works? What do you think would happen if at least once a day you took time to put these instructions into practice?
2. The way in which one leaves his first love for Christ is often a very subtle, undetectable process. Carefully review the section, "How Does One Leave His First Love?" and identify the common triggers/warning signs that accompany this spiritual tragedy.
3. Be honest with yourself and the Lord. Are you experiencing any of these symptoms presently in your life? If so, which one(s)?

PRACTICAL APPLICATION

But be ye doers of the word, and not hearers only, deceiving your own selves.
—James 1:22

1. God is so kind, generous, patient, and forgiving toward you. His mercies are new every morning (*see* Lamentations 3:22, 23). Take time right now to call to memory at least one thing God *has protected or kept you from* — and one way in which He *has tangibly blessed you.* Briefly describe each. (If more come to mind, wonderful! Take time to think on them and record them as well.)
2. Have you "left your first love"? Has the quality of your relationship with Jesus lost its awe and wonder? The Lord wants to restore the joy of His salvation in you! Here is a prayer you can pray to repent and receive His help: *"Lord, I ask that You would mentally take me back to the beginning of my relationship with You. By the power of Your Holy Spirit, refresh my memory of the joy and excitement of when I was first saved and filled with You. If I have drifted from You, my first love, please forgive me and help me return to doing the things I did when I first surrendered my life to You. I ask this in Jesus' name. Amen.*

---

[1] Rick Renner, *A Light in Darkness: Seven Messages to the Seven Churches*, Harrison House, Tulsa; Rick Renner Ministries, Tulsa. Second Edition. 2010, pp. 446-448.

LESSON 9

TOPIC

What Is True Repentance?

SCRIPTURES

1. **Revelation 2:1-5** — Unto the angel of the church of Ephesus write; These things saith he that holdeth the seven stars in his right hand, who walketh in the midst of the seven golden candlesticks; I know thy works, and thy labour, and thy patience, and how thou canst not bear them which are evil: and thou hast tried them which say they

are apostles, and are not, and hast found them liars: And hast borne, and hast patience, and for my name's sake hast laboured, and hast not fainted. Nevertheless I have somewhat against thee, because thou hast left thy first love. Remember therefore from whence thou art fallen, and repent, and do the first works; or else I will come unto thee quickly, and will remove thy candlestick out of his place, except thou repent.

2. **Matthew 27:3-5** — Then Judas, which had betrayed him, when he saw that he was condemned, repented himself, and brought again the thirty pieces of silver to the chief priests and elders, saying, I have sinned in that I have betrayed the innocent blood. And they said, What is that to us? See thou to that. And he cast down the pieces of silver in the temple, and departed, and went and hanged himself.
3. **Matthew 3:8** — Bring forth therefore fruits meet for repentance.

GREEK WORDS

1. "remember" — μ (*mneia*): denoted a written record used to memorialize a person's actions; often signified a statue, monument, or some type of memorial that was intended to be permanent; to remember, recollect, mention, commemorate, or memorialize
2. "whence" — ϖ (*pothen*): points back to a different place or a different time
3. "fallen" — ϖ ϖ (*pipto*): to fall; to collapse; to fall into a terrible predicament or into a worse state than one was in before; depicts someone who falls into some type of failure; a downward plummet; often used to depict a person who falls so hard that it appears he has fallen dead like a corpse; pictures a downfall from a presumed high and haughty position
4. "repent" — μ (*metanoeo*): pictures a change of mind that results in a complete, radical, total change of behavior; a decision to completely change or to entirely turn around in the way one is thinking, believing, or living; a decision to change one's thinking, believing, or actions; a decision to completely change or to entirely turn around in the way one is thinking, believing, or living; a total transformation affecting every part of a person's life, both inside and outside, resulting in a behavioral change
5. "remorse" — μ μ μ (*metamelomai*): expresses sorrow, mourning, or grief; to be seized with guilt; to be filled remorse or regret

6. "do" — ϖ (*poieo*): to do; to do creatively; to perform; it is the root word for "poet"

SYNOPSIS

Located in the lower part of Ephesus near the ancient harbor is the Church of Mary (also known as the Church of the Councils). Interestingly, this church is not dated back to the First Century, but to the Fourth Century, which is very important to note.

When Jesus was dying on the Cross, He looked at His mother and His beloved disciple John, saying to Mary, "…Woman, behold thy son!" (*see* John 19:26). Jesus then looked at John, affirming God's plan to him: "…Behold thy mother!…" (v. 27). Jesus committed the care of Mary to John, and from that moment forward, John took Mary into his home and cared for her until she passed away.

Years later, when John relocated from Israel to Asia, he brought Mary with him. Once they entered the new country, and their papers were processed, John and Mary moved to Ephesus where they became members of the church there. Three centuries later, the leaders of the church of Ephesus decided to build a church on the site where Mary and John had disembarked from the ship on which they had journeyed from Israel.

The significance of this brief history is this: Jesus appeared to John on the isle of Patmos and confronted the church of Ephesus because they had *left their first love* — they had lost their fervency and excitement for Christ that had burned in their hearts when they first came to Him. Jesus warned them to "…repent, and do the first works; or else I will come unto thee quickly, and will remove thy candlestick out of his place, except thou repent" (Revelation 2:5). Now think about it. For there to be a church in Ephesus that would later build the Church of Mary means that the Ephesian believers *did* repent and return to their first love! Their "candlestick" was *not* removed. Once they repented, they were revived, and the power of God continued to operate through them for hundreds of years. This clearly demonstrates the power of repentance.

The emphasis of this lesson:

The church of Ephesus had lost their first love for Christ, and He called them to repent. Although there is much confusion today among believers

regarding this subject, God is still calling His Church to repent. What is repentance? What *isn't* real, biblical repentance? And how do we repent once we understand the need for this act? This lesson answers these questions.

The Ephesians' Works Were Fully Known by the Lord

As Jesus began speaking to John in that cave on the isle of Patmos, He first turned John's attention to the church of Ephesus — the first church planted in Asia. It was the biggest, most powerful, and most influential church in the region. In Revelation 2:2, Christ declared: "I know thy works, and thy labour, and thy patience, and how thou canst not bear them which are evil: and thou hast tried them which say they are apostles, and are not, and hast found them liars."

We've learned that the word "know" is the Greek word *oida*, which means *to see*, *to behold*, or *to know something from personal observation*. What Jesus described about Ephesus was what He had seen with His own two eyes from walking among them and living in the very "midst" of the church — the Greek word *mesos*, meaning the church's *very heart*.

From verse 2, we also discovered that the church of Ephesus was an amazing work comprised of an amazing congregation of believers. They were hardworking, responsible, patiently enduring, and committed to doctrinal integrity. For all these characteristics, Christ commended them. In fact, He repeated His words of praise in Revelation 2:3 saying the Ephesians "...hast borne, and hast patience, and for my name's sake hast laboured, and hast not fainted."

The grammatical structure of this verse denotes that their godly actions had *not ceased*! On the contrary, they had been *continually* hardworking, *continually* responsible, *continually* patient, and *continually* committed to doctrinal integrity. They had endured in these traits and had not "fainted." The Greek word for "fainted" is *kopiao*, which means *to give up and give out*. The church of Ephesus did not faint even at times when they were weary to the point of exhaustion. Everything they did, they did for the right reason: they actually did all these things "for Christ's name's sake" (see v. 3).

Going Through the Motions

Yet when we come to Revelation 2:4, we hear Christ correcting the Ephesians. He had been commending them, but then He said, "Nevertheless I have somewhat against thee, because thou hast left thy first love."

"Nevertheless" is the Greek word *alla*, which indicates a break or shift in the text. It's as if Jesus was saying, "In spite of all the wonderful things I've just noted, there is something about you I need to address." He said, "I have somewhat against thee...." This word "against" is the Greek word *kata*, which describes *a downward mark or strike*. There was one strike against Ephesus that Jesus personally held, and it was one that deeply disturbed Him.

Why was Jesus so personally disturbed? He said, "...Because thou hast left thy first love." The grammatical structure here actually states, "Because your love — the first one — you have left it." When the Ephesian believers had first repented and surrendered their lives to Christ, they were overwhelmingly in love with Him. Like two young people who fall deeply in love with each other, the Ephesians were enamored with, excited about, in adoration of, and *totally committed* to Jesus! They willingly sacrificed everything for Him. Acts 19:17-20 records their zeal and how the power of God flowed through their lives. It was really quite amazing.

Then something happened. Over the more than 30 years since the Ephesian believers first came to Christ, things slowly and subtly changed. Although they continued to be actively involved in the machinery of ministry, they had "left" their early, passionate love for Jesus. Although they were going through the motions, their burning heart of devotion had all but disappeared.

They had "left" their first love. The word "left" is the Greek word *aphiemi*, which means *to involuntarily or voluntarily release something once held dear* — or *to unintentionally leave something or someone behind.* The word "left" does not mean to deliberately abandon. Instead, it signifies that over a period of time, the church of Ephesus became so involved in their activities and busy schedules that holy things became commonplace. What was once fresh and new was reduced to an ordinary, monotonous routine.

What did they need to do to make things right? Jesus told them in Revelation 2:5. "Remember therefore from whence thou art fallen, and repent, and do the first works; or else I will come unto thee quickly, and will remove thy candlestick out of his place, except thou repent."

The Remedy for Returning to One's First Love — Make the Effort *To Remember*

The first remedy for returning to one's first love for Christ, removing oneself from the rut of a passionless routine, is *to remember*. We covered that briefly in the last lesson. Revelation 2:5 says, "Remember therefore from whence thou art fallen, and repent, and do the first works; or else I will come unto thee quickly, and remove thy candlestick out of his place, except thou repent."

The word "remember" is the Greek word *mneia*. It denotes *a written record used to memorialize a person's past actions*. It often signified *a statue, a monument, or some type of memorial that was intended to be permanent*. It meant *to recollect, to commemorate, or to memorialize*. Interestingly, "remember" (*mneia*) is primarily the word for *a sepulcher of a tomb*.

If you think about it, a sepulcher is a place where memories are buried. The person who was laid to rest embodies a lifetime of memories shared with others. By using the word *mneia*, Jesus was basically saying, "There are things that you've forgotten — wonderful memories that are now buried under the busyness of your lives. And just as you would need to dig through the dirt to get to those who are buried with their memories, you need to dig through the clutter of your life — your activities, schedules, and routines, including the legitimate ones. Make the effort to dig down deep so you can get back to where you were when you first fell in love with Me. It's time for you to *remember*!"

Jesus continued elaborating on what He specifically wanted this group of believers to remember: "Remember therefore from *whence* thou art fallen..." (v. 5). The word "whence" is the Greek word *pothen*, which means *to point back to a different place or time*. Here, Jesus was saying, "I know you are sophisticated now, but let's dig down through all the years that have passed and get back to the beginning — that different place and time when your heart was ablaze with love for Me."

Christ wanted the Ephesians to remember from where they had "fallen." This is the Greek word *pipto*, and it describes *a collapse or a downward plummet*. It pictures *a downward fall from a formerly high position*. It is important to note that the tense of this verb describes a fall that has *already happened.* That is, Ephesus was not in the process of falling; they had already completely fallen. Although they looked great in the eyes of the church world, in Jesus' eyes, they had totally collapsed and plummeted from their place of the loving devotion and excitement toward Him that they once had.

Once these believers remembered from whence they had fallen, Jesus wanted them to "repent."

What Does It Mean To Repent?

"Repent" is the Greek word *metanoeo.* It is the compound of two words: the word *meta*, which carries the idea of *change*, and the word *noeo*, which is derived from the Greek word *nous* (the word to describe *the mind*). When *meta* and *noeo* are put together, they form the word *metanoeo*, which means *to think with a change* or *to think differently.*

Essentially, to "repent" (*metanoeo*) means *to make a change of mind that results in a complete, radical, total change of behavior.* It is *a decision to completely change or to entirely turn around in the way one is thinking, believing, or living.* True repentance is *a total transformation affecting every part of a person's life, both inside and out, resulting in behavioral change.*

It is important to note that inside this Greek word *metanoeo* is not one mention of shedding tears or showing emotions. In other words, repentance is *a decision.* This is why many evangelistic ministries record "decisions" for Christ when they win people into God's Kingdom — because surrendering one's life to Jesus is *a decision of one's will*! Certainly, there may be emotions involved, but they are *not* required — nor are they *proof* of genuine repentance.

It's also important to note that there is a difference between "repentance" and "remorse." Again, repentance describes a mental decision to turn the direction of one's life around in the way he thinks, believes, or lives. It results in a total transformation affecting every part of that person's life, both inside and out. On the other hand, a person who is remorseful usually displays deep emotion for his wrong behavior, but transformation never takes place. That person may feel badly for what happened and may even regret his actions — yet he makes no decision of the will to turn around from that behavior and to change.

Judas Was Remorseful, Not Repentant

In Matthew 27:3-5, Judas Iscariot gives us a sobering picture of what it means to be remorseful. The Scripture says, "Then Judas, which had betrayed him [Jesus], when he saw that he was condemned, repented himself, and brought again the thirty pieces of silver to the chief priests and elders, saying, I have sinned in that I have betrayed the innocent blood. And they said, What is that to us? See thou to that. And he cast down the pieces of silver in the temple, and departed, and went and hanged himself."

Notice the phrase "He repented himself." The word "repented" here is not *metanoeo*, which we just studied. This word "repented" is the Greek word *metamelomai*, and it describes *sorrow*, *mourning*, or *grief*. It means *to be seized with guilt*, *to be filled with remorse or regret*, or *to wallow in remorse*. Remorse denotes regret for being caught doing something wrong. It is sorrow for getting into trouble and having to pay the consequences, even the consequences of having guilty feelings over the person's own actions.

The word *metamelomai* depicts remorse that grips a person because of an act he committed that he knows was wrong. If this person was willing to *repent*, he could be forgiven and begin to change in that area where he committed a wrong. However, if he has no serious plans of repenting — stopping his sinful activity and rectifying what he has done — he might therefore be gripped with remorse. In other words, although he feels deep shame for what has done, he continues to do it anyway, resulting in an ongoing state of guilt. This guilt produces no change in his behavior or life.

Judas was *remorseful* — he "repented himself" for betraying Jesus, the innocent Lamb of God. He was seized with guilt and filled with regret for his actions. What was the outcome of his remorse? Judas went out and hung himself. When you truly repent, you don't go out and commit suicide. Instead, your decision to change results in a positive transformation that affects every part of your life, both inside and out.

True Repentance Produces Good Fruit

In Revelation 2:5, Jesus told the church of Ephesus, "Remember therefore from whence thou art fallen, and *repent*, and do the first works...." Notice He didn't say, "Cry, weep, and wail." He said, "Repent" — the Greek word *metanoeo*. Essentially, Jesus said, "I'm calling you to make a mental, willful decision to turn around and go back to doing the things you did when you first fell in love with Me."

When true repentance takes place, it produces good fruit. John the Baptist confirms this in Matthew 3:8 when he said, "Bring forth therefore fruits meet for repentance." Likewise, Jesus said, "Repent, and do the first works...." When you truly repent of wrong thinking or behavior, actions follow. You are going to begin to "do" something different, and the result will be good fruit in your life.

Friend, repentance can turn your life around. Repentance can save the day! The church of Ephesus experienced this firsthand, and *so can you!* If you're willing to hear and obey the voice of the Holy Spirit, He will go to work on your behalf. There is no sin so sinister that God won't forgive it, and there is no habit so deep-seated that He can't set you free. He's just waiting for you to *repent.* So if you're doing things that you know are wrong, make the decision today to change your direction, and God will activate His life-transforming power in *you.*

STUDY QUESTIONS

Study to shew thyself approved unto God, a workman that needeth not to be ashamed, rightly dividing the word of truth.
—2 Timothy 2:15

1. In your own words, briefly describe the difference between *repentance* and *remorse.* What is not required for repentance, but *almost always* accompanies remorse? What always results when you genuinely repent, but *never* happens when you're merely remorseful? (Consider the picture of repentance illustrated in 2 Chronicles 7:14.)
2. In Second Corinthians 7:10 and 11, Paul talked about *godly sorrow* and *worldly sorrow.* One brings about remorse and the other leads to true, fruit-bearing repentance. Carefully examine this passage and explain the difference between these two types of sorrow.

PRACTICAL APPLICATION

But be ye doers of the word, and not hearers only, deceiving your own selves.
—James 1:22

1. In light of the definitions of *repentance* and *remorse*, is there an area in your life where you have not truly repented, but have only been remorseful? If so, what is it? What signs indicate that true repentance has not taken place? What is the Holy Spirit prompting you to do regarding this situation?
2. The church of Ephesus was actively involved in the machinery of ministry. They were going through the motions, but missing the life-giving intimacy they once had with Jesus. Does this describe you? Has your Christian walk been reduced to a monotonous, boring routine? Be still before the Lord and ask Him, "Father, what needs to change in my thinking, believing, or living to enable me to enjoy a deeper, more meaningful level of intimacy with You?" Quietly listen. What is the Holy Spirit speaking to you?

LESSON 10

TOPIC

Who Were the Nicolaitans?

SCRIPTURES

1. **Revelation 2:1-5** — Unto the angel of the church of Ephesus write; These things saith he that holdeth the seven stars in his right hand, who walketh in the midst of the seven golden candlesticks; I know thy works, and thy labour, and thy patience, and how thou canst not bear them which are evil: and thou hast tried them which say they are apostles, and are not, and hast found them liars: And hast borne, and hast patience, and for my name's sake hast laboured, and hast not fainted. Nevertheless I have somewhat against thee, because thou hast left thy first love. Remember therefore from whence thou art fallen, and repent, and do the first works; or else I will come unto thee quickly, and will remove thy candlestick out of his place, except thou repent.
2. **Revelation 2:6, 7** — But this thou hast, that thou hatest the deeds of the Nicolaitans, which I also hate. He that hath an ear, let him hear what the Spirit saith unto the churches; to him that overcometh will I give to eat of the tree of life, which is in the midst of the paradise of God.

3. **Revelation 2:15** — So hast thou also them that hold the doctrine of the Nicolaitans, which thing I hate.

GREEK WORDS

1. "hatest" — μ (*miseo*): to abhor, or to find utterly repulsive; pictures a deep-seated animosity, intense hatred, or repugnance; depicts something objectionable or that causes one to feel disgust or repulsion; a deep-seated aversion; this is not just a case of dislike — it is actual hatred
2. "deeds" — (*erga*): some kind of action, deed, or activity; often it referred to a person's occupation, labor, or the things produced by someone's effort or life; a person's line of work, career, or profession; denoted the result of hard work or hard labor; this word is so all-encompassing that it also pictures actions, beliefs, and conduct
3. "Nicolaitans" — (*nikolaos*): a proper Greek name that means one who conquers and subdues people; to conquer and subdue people
4. "hate" — μ (*miseo*): to abhor, or to find utterly repulsive; pictures a deep-seated animosity, intense hatred, or repugnance; depicts something objectionable or that causes one to feel disgust or repulsion; a deep-seated aversion; this is not just a case of dislike — it is actual hatred
5. "overcometh" — (*nikao*): pictures a victor, champion, or one who possesses some type of superiority; can be translated to conquer, defeat, master, overcome, overwhelm, surpass, or be victorious; often used in Greek literature to portray athletes who had mastered their sport and ultimately reigned supreme as champions in the games; could also describe a military victory of one foe against the other; to be permanently and consistently undeterred in one's efforts to overcome and to obtain a lasting victory

SYNOPSIS

About 2,000 years ago in the lower district of ancient Pergamum stood the Egyptian temple of Isis and Serapis. At that time, there were many Egyptians living in Asia. They tended to congregate in major Asian cities — especially in Pergamum. This temple was where they worshiped. Today it is called the Red Hall (or the Red Court) due to the red bricks used in its construction. First Century believers would not enter such places because they didn't want to be tempted to return to the sin practiced by the people insides its walls. Therefore, they shunned pagan temples.

However, there was a group of professing Christian teachers called the Nicolaitans who did not hold to the same standard. "We don't need to live so strictly separated," these teachers said. "These pagans are good people, and we need to spend time with them and go to their temples. If we befriend them, maybe we can win them to Christ."

Basically, the Nicolaitans condoned *compromise*, and Jesus was totally against their deeds and doctrines — so was the church of Ephesus. In Revelation 2:6 and 15, Jesus said He "hated" what the Nicolaitans were propagating. Since Jesus hates compromise, we should hate it too.

The emphasis of this lesson:

Learn what the doctrine of the Nicolaitans was in the Early Church and see why Jesus and the church of Ephesus hated it. You will also discover four primary indicators that confirm how and where Nicolatianism is still manifesting in the world today — including inside the Church.

What We've Learned So Far

As we have learned throughout the last several lessons, in Revelation 2:1, Jesus was speaking "unto the angel of the Church of Ephesus…." The word "angel" is the Greek word *angelos*, which means *the pastor or overseer of the church*. By speaking to the pastor of the church first, Christ shows us that He never bypasses, but *honors*, the spiritual authority He has established. When He has a message to speak to the local church, especially if that message is a rebuke, the pastor will be the first to hear it.

We also discovered in Revelation 2:1 where Jesus was and what He was doing when He spoke His message to the pastor of the church of Ephesus. He said, "These things saith he that holdeth the seven stars in his right hand, who walketh in the midst of the seven golden candlesticks."

The word "walketh" is the Greek word *peripateo*. This is a compound of the word *peri*, meaning *around*, and the word *pateo*, meaning *to walk*. When these two words are put together to form *peripateo*, it signifies that Jesus was walking around the church, getting a good exterior view of what was happening. When that was no longer enough, He came *inside* the "midst" of the church.

The word "midst" is the Greek word *mesos*. It means *to be right in the very heart or gut of a thing*. Christ was walking inside the very heart of the church. In fact, the word "walketh" (*peripateo*) describes *one who regularly or habitually walks in one place*. Thus, Jesus was living and walking habitually in the church.

From His inside vantage point, Jesus was able to see *everything* about the Ephesians. That is why in Revelation 2:2 He said, "I know thy works…." The word "know" is the Greek word *oida*, which means *to see, behold, or know something from personal observation*. Jesus personally observed the Ephesians' "works" — the Greek word *erga*, describing *the totality of one's actions, deeds, and activities*. Essentially, Jesus said, "I know everything there is to know about you; I've seen it all with My own two eyes. Nothing has escaped Me."

Jesus also commended the Ephesian believers. "I know thy works, and thy labour, and thy patience, and how thou canst not bear them which are evil: and thou hast tried them which say they are apostles, and are not, and hast found them liars" (Revelation 2:2). These believers were very hardworking, patient, and enduring. Christ applauded them for that and for their love of doctrinal purity, as well as their efforts to test those who claimed to be apostles. Their diligent investigations revealed that many were actually liars.

All the attributes Jesus recognized were *ongoing* practices. He confirmed this in Revelation 2:3 when He stated, "And *hast* borne, and *hast* patience, and for my name's sake *hast* laboured, and *hast* not fainted." In the Greek, this actually says, "You have been *continually* responsible, *continually* patient, and *continually* hardworking. You didn't just do these things in the beginning. You've *continued* in them all."

Then Jesus said, "…And hast not *faint*ed." The word "fainted" is the Greek word *kopiao*, which means *to give in and give out after being weary to the point of exhaustion*. This is exactly what the church of Ephesus did *not* do. Instead of fainting, they continued in all these good works, and Jesus commended them for it.

There was one strike against Ephesus. Jesus said in Revelation 2:4, "Nevertheless I have somewhat *against* thee…." The word "against" is the Greek word *kata*, and it describes *a downward mark or a strike against*. Basically, Jesus said, "In spite of all the good things I've just recognized about you, there's something I've seen that's not good, and it is a strike against you. It's something I hold personally against you."

What was that one thing? Jesus said, "…Because thou hast left thy *first* love" (Revelation 2:4). As we've noted, the Greek structure of this phrase actually says, "Because your love — the first one — you have left." The phrase "the first one" could be translated as *early love*. He was referring to what they were like when they first came to Him and had fallen in love with Him.

The Ephesian congregation had "left" their first love. The word "left" is the Greek word *aphiemi*, which is not to deliberately abandon a thing. Instead, it is *a voluntary release of something once held dear*. Although these believers were working hard, patiently enduring, and protecting doctrinal integrity, they had been reduced to going through the motions. They were trafficking in the *machinery* of ministry, but had let the intimacy they once shared with Jesus slip through their fingers.

Therefore, Jesus urged them to "…*remember* from whence thou art fallen, and repent…" (Revelation 2:5). The word "remember" is the Greek word *mneia*, which is the Greek word for *a sepulcher or tomb*. By using this word *mneia*, Jesus was saying, "The precious memories you had with Me when you first welcomed Me into your life have all become buried under the clutter of so many years of activity. But dig back to the beginning, removing all the dirt of activity so that you can resurrect those early memories you once held dear."

They were to remember from "whence" they had fallen. The word "whence" is the Greek word *pothen*, which *denotes pointing back to an earlier or different time and place*. Jesus was saying, "Go back to the very beginning to remember what you were like when you first came to Me." Acts 19 tells us that the church of Ephesus was aflame with the fire of the Holy Spirit during the time of their "early love" for the Savior.

Nevertheless, they had "fallen" from that place and time. The word "fallen" is the Greek term *pipto*, and it describes *a downfall or plummet that has already taken place*. It is not something about to happen or in the process of happening. In comparison to the high level of intimacy the church of Ephesus once walked in, they had already completely fallen.

Jesus called this congregation to repent and to do the first works. The word "repent" is *metanoeo* in Greek, and it describes *a change of mind*. It is *a decision* and has nothing to do with emotions. By using "repent" (*metanoeo*), Jesus was saying, "Make a decision to change your thinking. Turn around and go back to the way you were in your relationship with Me."

Then what did Jesus tell them to do? The "first works." That phrase, "first works" in the Greek is *prota erga*, which means *the first or early works*, *deeds, or activities*. "First works" could actually be interpreted as "the actions that were indicative of you at the first" or, "the things that were indicative of you when you first started."

Ephesian Believers Hated the Deeds of the Nicolaitans

Interestingly, in Revelation 2:6, Christ moved away from correction and offered another word of praise for the Ephesian believers. He said, "But this thou hast, that thou hatest the deeds of the Nicolaitans, which I also hate."

The phrase, "But this thou hast," could better be translated, "But you do have this one thing really in your favor." What was this one thing? They hated the deeds of the Nicolaitans. Although the word "hate" is a very strong word, it is important to see what it means and the context of how it is being used.

"Hatest" is the Greek word *miseo*, which means *to hate*, *abhor*, or *find utterly repulsive*. It is *a deep-seated animosity*, *intense hatred*, or *repugnance*. *Miseo* depicts *something objectionable* or *something that causes one to feel disgust or repulsion*. Make no mistake, this *deep-seated aversion* is not just a case of dislike — it is actual hatred.

But notice Jesus did *not* say the Ephesian believers hated the Nicolaitans themselves, nor did He that say that *He* hated the Nicolaitans. Christ does not hate people, and we are not to hate people either — regardless of their behavior or whether they agree with us or not. Jesus and the church of Ephesus hated the *deeds* of the Nicolaitans. We can hate the deeds, teachings, and influences of ungodly people, but we are never to hate the people themselves.

The word "deeds" in this verse is the Greek term *erga*, which is the same word for "works." Again, it describes *some kind of action*, *deed*, or *activity*. It is a word so all-encompassing that it also pictures one's *actions*, *beliefs*, and *conduct.* The influence of the Nicolaitans was very negative and harmful, and the church of Ephesus as well as Jesus absolutely hated it.

Who Were the Nicolaitans?

You can get an understanding of who the Nicolaitans were from the meaning of their name. The word "Nicolaitan" is from the Greek word *Nikolaos*, which is the compound of two words. The word *nike* means *to conquer*, and the word *laos* is where we get the word *laity*, which describes *the people*. When the words *nike* and *laos* are combined, the word *Nikolaos* is formed, which means *to conquer and subdue people* or *one who conquers or subdues the laity.*

Apparently, the Nicolaitans' actions and teachings were having a conquering, subjugating effect on the people of God. The end result of their "deeds" was defeated believers. Jesus hated it. He was absolutely repulsed by what they were doing, and so were the people of the church of Ephesus.

Some of the Early Church fathers also commented on the deeds of the Nicolaitans, describing them as "a heretical group that taught there was nothing wrong with serving Christ while simultaneously participating in pagan practices." In other words, the Nicolaitans' motto seemed to be, "Let's compromise. Instead of living separate from the world or in opposition to the world's ways, let's make adjustments that enable us to fit in and be accepted." The Nicolaitans believed and taught that it was acceptable to go to pagan temples and make sacrifices to pagan gods if it would buy some peace with pagan neighbors.

Jesus hated that mindset, and He especially loathed it because it was appealing to new Christians. Christ had called them to a life of separation (*see* 2 Corinthians 6:14-18). Yet, these new, young believers became confused by the Nicolaitan philosophy, which declared, "Hey, you can think and act like a pagan and still be a Christian. You don't have to live a life separated from the things of the world. You are free to compromise."

When people first surrendered their lives to Christ, many of their family members were still entrenched in a pagan lifestyle. Compromise made their lives much easier. This is what the Nicolaitans were endorsing, and it was utterly detestable to Jesus. To be clear, Christ loved the Nicolaitans. He loved them so much that He died for them. What He hated was their teachings that were leading people astray.

Are There Nicolaitans in the Modern Church?

Yes, the spirit of the Nicolaitans is alive and well in people today. It is seen in the lives of spiritual leaders who seek a truce with the world and its people under the guise of *inclusiveness* and *compromise*. Sadly, some of these leaders once held strong biblical positions. Over time, however, they have reshaped their beliefs to reflect the changing moral climate of society. In the process, they have produced a gospel very different from the one presented in the Bible.

The following are four primary indicators that confirm modern Nicolaitanism.

1. **No emphasis on holy living and separation from the world**. Rather than living separate from the world, modern Nicolaitanism dresses itself in the guise of *inclusiveness*. They infer that we need to accept and embrace everyone — including their lifestyle choices. For example, there are some denominational churches that fully accept and embrace sexual lifestyle choices that are contrary to Scripture. Ultimately, modern Nicolaitanism does away with the notion of sin and the need for repentance.
2. **No emphasis on the doctrinal teachings of the Bible**. In this case, modern Nicolaitanism dresses itself up in the guise of *progressiveness*. They dismiss much of the Bible as too restrictive or exclusive of other people's beliefs. Instead of being a guide to absolute truth, Scripture is used merely as a reference book for motivational sermons, inspirational ideas, or life principles to build a better marriage or business.

   This trend is so rampant in the Church today that the basic tenants of the Christian faith are largely unknown by churchgoers — especially by those who are younger. Basic Bible doctrines such as sin, salvation, the virgin birth, the sinless nature of Christ, holiness, and eternal judgment are unknown by many. Modern Nicolaitanism has replaced these foundational teachings with social justice and social action. They aim to be politically correct and make the masses feel good about themselves. They contend that the Bible is never to be used as a standard, against which to judge others' actions or lifestyles — *or* to imply that anyone else is wrong about anything.
3. **No emphasis on truth or absolute biblical authority.** Modern Nicolaitanism also dresses itself in the guise of being *open-minded*. Its proponents claim it is unfair and unjust to allow beliefs alone to be

the absolute foundation of truth. They allege we are to always make allowances that we may be wrong in what we believe or that others may be equally right with their different, unbiblical approach.

This mindset has infiltrated and damaged the Church so deeply that it is estimated that more than half of evangelical Christians do not believe in absolute truth. Just have an open, honest conversation with believers under the age of 25, and this will be confirmed. Modern Nicolaitanism has produced a negative view of people who adhere to the Bible as absolute truth.

4. **No exclusionary belief that Christ alone is the way to Heaven**. A fourth major indicator of modern Nicolaitanism comes in the guise of *tolerance*. Here the assertion is that everyone has a piece of the truth. This levels the playing field, making Christianity simply one truth among other truths.

   If Nicolaitanism is followed to its logical conclusion, it eventually leads to universalism, which is the belief that everyone, including the devil himself, will ultimately be reconciled to God. In other words, under the "tolerance" rule, there are many roads that lead to Heaven, or to the same eternal destination, and everyone is free to find his own way. According to this mindset, it is simply unintelligent nonsense to declare that Jesus is *the* way, *the* truth, and *the* life — yet Scripture plainly states that He *is* and that there is no other name under Heaven by which we can be eternally saved (*see* John 14:6; Acts 4:12).

   When the doctrine of modern Nicolaitanism is embraced, it produces a powerless, weakened version of Christianity where sin is tolerated, separation from the world is ignored, and the need for repentance is disregarded. This is why Jesus hated the deeds and doctrine of the Nicolaitans, and it's why He commended the church of Ephesus for hating it too.

Do You Have an Ear To Hear?

Since Jesus had a hatred for the deeds and doctrine of the Nicolaitans, we, too, should hate this horrible doctrine. Jesus called all Christians to take decisive action in this matter just after He finished addressing the issue of the Nicolaitans. In Revelation 2:7, He said, "He that hath an ear, let him hear what the Spirit saith unto the churches; to him that overcometh will I give to eat of the tree of life, which is in the midst of the paradise of God."

Not everyone has an ear to hear what the Lord is saying. But for those who do have an ear to hear and obey, He will give the right to eat of the tree of life. That includes you! You are called to overcome — overcome your own fleshly ways, your environment, the enemy, and everything that contradicts or compromises the Word of God.

He said, "…To him that overcometh will I give to eat of the tree of life, which is in the midst of the paradise of God" (Revelation 2:7). The word "overcometh" is the Greek word *nikao*, and it describes *a victor*, *a champion*, or *one who possesses some type of superiority*. It can be translated *to conquer*, *defeat*, *master*, *overcome*, *overwhelm*, *surpass*, or *be victorious*.

This is God's call for every single believer — including you!

STUDY QUESTIONS

Study to shew thyself approved unto God, a workman that needeth not to be ashamed, rightly dividing the word of truth.
— 2 Timothy 2:15

1. The word "Nicolaitan" is from the Greek word *Nikolaos*, which means *to conquer and subdue people* or *one who conquers or subdues the laity.* In your own words, briefly explain the deeds and doctrine of the Nicolaitans and why Jesus despised their teachings so greatly. (Consider Mark 9:42 and Romans 14:19-21.)
2. Take some time to meditate on God's words through the apostle Paul in Second Corinthians 6:14-18. What is the Holy Spirit speaking to you in this passage about living a life of separation? (Also consider Ephesians 5:11; 2 Thessalonians 3:6 and James 1:27.)
3. The spirit of the Nicolaitans is alive and well in the world today. It is seen in the lives of spiritual leaders who seek a truce with the world in the name of *inclusivism, progressivism, tolerance*, and being *open-minded.* List the four major indicators of modern Nicolaitanism.

PRACTICAL APPLICATION

But be ye doers of the word, and not hearers only, deceiving your own selves.
— James 1:22

1. Most First Century Christians chose *not* to enter pagan temples. They had been supernaturally delivered from sin by the power of God's Spirit, and they did not want to be enslaved by it again. Look back on your "pre-Christ" days. What are some of the sin practices you have been delivered from? Be honest: Is there a place you have been frequenting that is putting you in jeopardy of falling back into an ungodly lifestyle? If so, where? Take steps now to ask God to forgive you. Then begin *to put space between you and that place.*
2. The Nicolaitans condoned compromising with the world. Things that God clearly called sin in His Word they claimed were acceptable. Modern Nicolaitans continue this line of thinking and teaching today. Is there a spiritual leader you've been listening to that you realize falls into this category? Likewise, is there an area in which you have unknowingly adopted the mindset of the Nicolaitans, downplaying the seriousness of sin? If so, in what area? How does this lesson change your perspective?

Notes

Notes

Notes

CLAIM YOUR FREE RESOURCE!

As a way of introducing you further to the teaching ministry of Rick Renner, we would like to send you FREE of charge his teaching, "How To Receive a Miraculous Touch From God" on CD or USB format.

In His earthly ministry, Jesus commonly healed *all* who were sick of *all* their diseases. In this profound message, learn about the manifold dimensions of Christ's wisdom, goodness, power, and love toward all humanity who came to Him in faith with their needs.

☑ **YES, I want to receive Rick Renner's monthly teaching letter!**

Simply scan the QR code to claim this resource or go to:
renner.org/claim-your-free-offer

renner.org

facebook.com/rickrenner • facebook.com/rennerdenise

youtube.com/rennerministries • youtube.com/deniserenner

instagram.com/rickrrenner • instagram.com/rennerministries_
instagram.com/rennerdenise